Murderous Minds

Stories of Real-Life Murderers
that Escaped the Headlines

Murderous Minds Volume 3

Ryan Becker, Kurtis-Giles Veysey, and True Crime Seven

TRUE CRIME 7

Copyright © 2020 by Sea Vision Publishing, LLC

All Rights Reserved.

No part of this publication may be reproduced, distributed, or transmitted in any form or by any means, including photocopying, recording, electronic or mechanical methods, without the prior written permission of the publisher, except in the case of brief quotations embodied in critical reviews and certain other non-commercial uses permitted by copyright law.

Much research, from a variety of sources, has gone into the compilation of this material. We strive to keep the information up-to-date to the best knowledge of the author and publisher; the materials contained herein is factually correct. Neither the publisher nor author will be held responsible for any inaccuracies.

ISBN: 978-1790892129

Table of Contents

Table of Contents *5*

Introduction *11*

I: Joachim Kroll *19*

II: Alfred Packer *51*

III: Boone Helm *77*

IV: Tsutomu Miyazaki *89*

V: Peter Niers *102*

VI: Alexander Spesivtsev *116*

Conclusion *128*

Acknowledgements *131*

About True Crime Seven *157*

Explore the Stories of
The Murderous Minds

A Note

From True Crime Seven

Hi there!

Thank you so much for picking up our book! Before you continue your exploration into the dark world of killers, we wanted to take a quick moment to explain the purpose of our books.

Our goal is to simply explore and tell the stories of various killers in the world: from unknown murderers to infamous serial killers. Our books are designed to be short and inclusive; we want to tell a good scary true story that anyone can enjoy regardless of their reading level.

That is why you won't see too many fancy words or complicated sentence structures in our books. Also, to prevent the typical cut and dry style of true crime books, we try to keep the narrative easy to follow while incorporating fiction style storytelling. As to information, we often find ourselves with too little or too much. So, in terms of research material and content, we always try to include what further helps the story of the killer.

Lastly, we want to acknowledge that, much like history, true crime is a subject that can often be interpreted differently. Depending on the topic and your upbringing, you might agree or disagree with how we present a story. We understand disagreements are inevitable. That is why we added this note so hopefully, it can help you better understand our position and goal.

Now without further ado, let the exploration to the dark begin!

Introduction

BLOODSHED AND CANNIBALISM WERE FREQUENT aspects of religious rituals throughout history. So why does the word "cannibalism" unnerve us so much today? Perhaps because there is no longer a need to consume our fellow man in order to survive and relying less as a whole on what we now perceive as superstitious rituals.

When we do have to make a choice between eating one of our own or dying of starvation, it seems our survival instincts override our ethics. It's a horrifying thought to be left with no other choice than to eat another human, but throughout history, it has been one people have had to make.

Many reports of survival cannibalism surfaced during World War II. During this dark time, victims of the Holocaust often resorted to cannibalism. So, too, did German soldiers during the eight hundred- and seventy-two-day Siege of Leningrad. After having eaten all animals in the area, survivors trapped in the city began to resort to cannibalism in the winter of 1941-1942. German prisoners of war in Siberia, being underfed, also ate others out of necessity.

If we go only a little further back in history, we'll also discover the Donner Party, who were stranded in the Sierra Nevada Mountains in 1846. Those who died of exposure to the elements and starvation were eaten by the others.

Repeated rescue attempts managed to save forty-five people, but when the final rescue party arrived, only one man remained. The man was Lewis Keseburg, who, when the rest of the party began resorting to cannibalism, took a young boy with him to bed one night and brought his corpse to the rest of the party the next morning for butchering.

When the rescue party arrived, Keseburg was lying amidst the wreckage of the camp, with a simmering pot of human liver and lungs. Keseburg informed the rescuers that the liver belonged to the other final survivor, Mrs. Donner, who was "the best [he had] ever tasted." Mrs. Donner had been healthy just weeks earlier, which made Keseburg's allegations she had died from natural causes seem suspicious. Though he was arrested and tried for the murder, he claimed he had only resorted to cannibalism out of desperation, just like the rest of the party, and was subsequently released. He went on to open a steak house.

More recently, a tale of survivor cannibalism came out of the Andes Mountains. A passenger plane traveling from Argentina to Chile crashed high in the mountain range, at an altitude of twenty-three thousand feet. Due to the subzero temperatures, there was no edible vegetation. Several passengers perished during the crash or shortly thereafter. Those who survived were abandoned in the desolate landscape.

Weeks passed, and the survivors began to grow hungry. They were faced with the grim realization that to survive, they must eat the remains of those who had died in the crash—perhaps even more unthinkable because the victims were their own loved ones. Some refused to do so and eventually died the slow death of starvation. Those who ate their companions managed to survive seventy days before finally being rescued, though their numbers were very few. Only sixteen out of forty-five passengers had lived.

Other times, one may decide to eat his fellow men not out of desperation, or even out of primitive ritual, but for reasons known only to himself: simply enjoying consuming human flesh. Occasionally, such was the case with Liver-Eating Johnson in the 1880s, in his desire for revenge.

John "Liver-Eating" Johnson's wife and child had been killed by Crow Indians, so, whenever Johnson happened upon a Crow camp, he would attack it, kill the Indians, and eat only their livers.

Or, perhaps more disturbing, would be the case of Sawney Bean, who, contrary to the belief of some, did, in fact, exist and was well-documented. Sawney Bean and his numerous offspring, conceived via incest, lived in a coastal cave in Scotland. The family made their living by attacking, murdering, and robbing individuals or small groups. They would then eat their victims' flesh or pickle and hang the unconsumed flesh in their cave. The clothes and valuables taken from their victims would be sold in the Edinburgh region.

In recent years, the act of consensual cannibalism has been in the public eye. Following cases such as that of Armin Meiwes and Detlev Guensel, who both committed consensual cannibalism in

Germany. A debate arose as to what punishment to deliver in such a case, and whether or not the act was truly consensual.

Can it really be consensual, and acceptable, if the consequences are deadly? Can the consent be valued when it is coming from someone who is emotionally unstable, or who may have underlying psychiatric issues? Should such a dark, morbid desire be treated as any other desire and, therefore, should the consent be valuable?

Despite the fact that Armin Meiwes was sentenced to life in prison—originally, it was eight and a half years, but the trial was reopened—the answers to these questions have not been answered. These cases of "consensual cannibalism" often begin in online forums, where people such as Meiwes put what is quite basically a "wanted" ad for a human dinner.

The plan often goes awry, usually when the one to be eaten changes their mind and calls the police. Though, with Meiwes and his willing victim, Bernd Brandes, they actually went all the way, with Meiwes filming a two-hour video of him mutilating the man, sharing the flesh with him, then eventually killing and butchering him.

The popular cannibal forum Cannibal Café has been shut down due to the number of attention cases such as these have gotten. Vorarephilia, or, the deriving of pleasure—typically sexual—from the thought of being eaten, eating others, or watching people or animals eat each other, is a rare phenomenon, but forums such as the Cannibal Café have brought people who experience this together, and, apparently, the results are often abysmal.

Many have often wondered what exactly human flesh tastes like. One man, reporter William Beuhler Seabrook, also had the same question and satisfied his thirst for knowledge by obtaining, from a hospital intern, a chunk of human flesh from someone who had died in a car accident. After he cooked and ate the meat, he stated that it tasted very much like veal, and most people would not be able to tell the difference. He also expressed that it was slightly tougher than prime veal, as well as a little stringy, and it did not have any recognizable traits.

The stories in this book will look at two reasons for cannibalism: cannibalism in order to survive, and the eating of humans for personal pleasure.

Frequently, there are psychological factors as to why one would engage in cannibalism; typically, the desire to eat another is caused by a need for control over the victim or for a part of the victim to always remain with the perpetrator.

In survival situations, cannibalism is resorted to due to no other choice. This book is presented in a historical context, and some of the cases presented in it are now regarded as legendary. Cannibals such as Jeffery Dahmer or Albert Fish may be familiar to anyone who studies true crime, but, as with always in this series, this book is comprised of lesser-known murderers.

In this book, you will read about:

- Joachim Kroll: a man who loved the taste of human flesh almost as much as he loved his child-sized dolls, which he would use not only to entice little girls but to practice strangling them, usually while masturbating. Despite his low IQ, Kroll managed to evade law enforcement for two decades, during which time he terrorized the Ruhr region of Germany, preying on young women and girls he thought looked tasty.
- Alfred Packer: a man whose exact crimes have been debated for nearly a century and a half. Packer might not have slaughtered his companions outright during their expedition through the frigid San Juan Mountains of Colorado, but he certainly made a glutton of himself on their flesh.

- Boone Helm: one of the most heartless and feared killers of the Old West. Helm was not afraid to take the life of anyone he so pleased, nor was he afraid to die himself. Helm boasted, "Many's the poor devil I've killed, at one time or another...and the time has been that I've been obliged to feed on some of 'em."
- Tsutomu Miyazaki: a man who had as much of an interest in little girls as he did in both pornographies featuring them and manga. Though he had few victims and only consumed one of them, he nevertheless terrorized Saitama prefecture as badly as he terrorized his victims' families.
- Peter Niers: a medieval murderer, cannibal, thief, and practitioner of black magic. His confession was made under torture and, though shocking, was not nearly as bizarre as the ballads weaved about his supernatural abilities or his three-day, barbaric execution.
- Alexander Spesivtsev: described as an "intellectual" by law enforcement, and a published author of philosophy, he decided to show his displeasure with the newly-established democracy of Russia by killing and eating street children. With the help of his mother, he committed the vilest acts, and only caught the attention of law enforcement when a pipe got clogged up.

I
Joachim Kroll

ON SATURDAY, JULY 3, 1976, A YOUNG MAN WITH dark-blond, curly hair, a broad, honest face, massive, square physique stumbled backward out of a narrow, smelly toilet on the fourth floor of a block of apartments in Laar, West Germany, and hit the ground in a dead faint.

This astonished those who observed the incident because the man was Detective Max Riese of the Duisburg Police. If any place in Germany was least likely to have a fainting cop, it was Duisburg, in the Ruhr region. And if any cop were least likely to faint, it was Riese. A twenty-year veteran of the force, he had seen the worst men could to do one another. Or so he thought.

An area known for its mining industry, the Ruhr region encompasses fifty industrial cities and is often referred to as the Iron Triangle. Due to its large industrial role, it is a heavily populated, and also incredibly polluted area. Like something most people would only associate with a place such as Chernobyl, soot, and sulfuric acid regularly fall from the sky, coloring the waterways bright shades of yellow and green, rendering local streams devoid of life. Wildlife, the few able to exist in the toxic environment, are poisonous and considered inedible, like most forms of plant life.

Although the Ruhr region is incapable of sustaining itself by farming due to its poisonous and inhospitable environment, Germany is nonetheless proud of the wealth its mining industry has brought to the country, if not to the individuals themselves. Citizens must often go to extreme measures and think in ways that are adaptive to their harsh surroundings in order to survive.

One of the region's denizens had honed his method of stalking and dispatching his prey for over two decades.

It was the result of these practices which brought the policeman to his knees outside the small bathroom that July day in 1976. For over twenty years, forty-three-year-old Joachim Kroll had patiently stalked his victims, often going years at a time between killings, a practice which defies most notions regarding serial killers and "cooling off" periods between murders. Kroll was a strange but beloved member of his community, and police had just stumbled onto the evidence of his depraved practices and no one was prepared for what they discovered about "Uncle Joachim."

Joachim Georg Kroll was born on April 17, 1933, in Hindenburg, Province of Upper Silesia. He was a small, weak child and known to wet the bed—according to some reports, even into adulthood. He tended to struggle in school and ended up only making it to the third grade. Much later, upon being examined by psychiatrists, it was found he only had an IQ of seventy-six, making him mentally handicapped.

Once he was an adult, he was known to love the company of children, although it would later be discovered his adoration of little girls went far beyond that of a nurturing desire. The children in his neighborhood referred to him as "Uncle Joachim," because he was so kind to them, and because his little apartment was filled with various toys, dolls, and candy. Joachim was viewed as a friendly man who would invite all the neighborhood children into his home. He loved the attention from the little girls, who, in turn, loved his collection of child-sized dolls. Unbeknownst to the girls or their families, "Uncle Joachim" would use these dolls to practice strangling little girls. Nobody knew, either, of his blow-up sex dolls, which he would also strangle.

The families in the neighborhood in Duisburg thought of the little, dingy-looking brown-eyed man as being a sweet fellow who just wanted a family of his own. They trusted him to go on walks with their young girls, and, despite what Kroll did to numerous other young girls who became victims of his hidden sadistic side, these children always came home safely and happily, usually full of the sweets he would offer them.

Although a bit dim-witted, adults felt the time he spent lavishing affection and gifts on the neighborhood children was in an effort to fill the lonely void his mother's death had left in the life of this childless bachelor. Little did they know that, after his mother's death in 1955, something snapped inside Kroll, horrible desires which earned him the names "Ruhr Cannibal," "Ruhr Hunter," and "Duisburg Man-Eater."

In his childhood, after World War II was over, Joachim Kroll and his family moved to North Rhine-Westphalia. Then, Kroll's closest confidante, his mother, died when he was twenty-two. Three weeks after her death, lonely and desperate for human interaction, Kroll went in search of something: a girl. He took a train a short way, before exiting at a random stop. He then continued on foot, before finally encountering nineteen-year-old Irmgard Strehl. She was a vision of blonde loveliness dressed all in green, a youth who had also taken a train, and was now walking to her destination, the nearby village of Herrenstein, less than a mile away.

Kroll found her very attractive, and when he had encountered her on the road, he asked her if she would like to take a walk in the woods. Irmgard agreed. Making the same fateful mistake many others would in the future, she felt the little man couldn't possibly be a threat, and he certainly seemed friendly enough. After walking only a short distance and out of sight from prying eyes, Kroll attempted to kiss Irmgard, but she resisted. Kroll, angered by her actions, stabbed her four times in the neck. Then, he grabbed her by her bloody throat and strangled her. Once Irmgard stopped struggling and the life left her eyes, Kroll raped her body. Then, he cut her abdomen open, spilling her guts as though she were a pig.

When Irmgard failed to arrive at her parents' house for lunch, they immediately sensed something was amiss. A search party, which included almost every able-bodied person of the small hamlet, was formed by her worried mother and father. The search did not last long. On the same day she went missing, February 8, 1955, Irmgard Strehl's body was found by three in the afternoon, partially hidden by snow-covered brush that surrounded it, only a few hundred feet from the road.

There was a large amount of semen in her vagina, as well as on her abdomen and pubic hair, a finding which helped Kroll evade detection. Upon noting this unusual finding, officials first believed the crime was committed by a group, or gang, due to the significant amount of seminal evidence. Residents, especially single women, were warned if they must travel alone, to avoid groups of young men. No one had any idea that it was a single individual to blame for the crime. Only after he was arrested decades later would authorities learn of Kroll's nearly insatiable sexual appetite and the copious amounts of semen he produced.

Twenty-four-year-old Klara Frieda Tesmer was yet another blonde whom Kroll encountered and desired in the same way he had desired his first victim. It was June 16, 1959, and Klara was out walking. Years later, in his confession, Kroll detailed how he had taken her by the arm, but she had resisted and tried to pull away. Enraged by her rebuff, Kroll reacted by hitting her on the head. While Kroll attempted to undress Klara, they struggled and the two rolled down a small incline, off the road and out of view. Kroll decided to simply strangle Klara to death, before making any attempt to have sexual relations with her.

Once he was done, Kroll decided to try something new with the lifeless body. Klara, he thought, looked positively delicious, so he carved pieces of flesh from her buttocks and thighs with a long-bladed knife, wrapped them in a piece of fabric ripped from his victim's dress, and took them home with him. To eat.

Klara's body was later discovered by some young boys riding their bicycles. Like Irmgard Strehl, Klara's body was found raped and strangled in a small patch of woods outside the city limits. Having no reason to believe the murder of Klara was connected with the murder four years prior, the crimes would not be linked for many years.

In their search for Klara's killer, and going on the assumption the murder was an isolated occurrence, police zeroed in on a man they felt was most likely the perpetrator. Heinrich Ott, a thirty-seven-year-old mechanic, was arrested for Klara's murder. The police had come to suspect him in a series of sex murders that had taken place in the surrounding area in the years preceding Klara's death.

Perhaps he was guilty of some of the killings he was accused of committing, but it is just as likely that Joachim Kroll had murdered some, or all, of the women. Ott certainly was not guilty in the death of Klara Tesmer, but police did not know that, nor did they know about Kroll. When Heinrich Ott committed suicide by hanging himself in his cell before he ever went to trial, this was all the proof law enforcement and citizens needed of his guilt.

Manuela Knodt was just sixteen when, on July 26, 1959, her life was snuffed out. It had been a little over a month since Kroll had murdered Klara Tesmer, and the crime occurred twenty miles away, in a town called Bredeney. This murder, like the first two, was also viewed as an isolated incident, even though she was strangled and raped, much like the other victims. Also, as with the earlier murders, an enormous amount of semen was found on the victim's body. Again, local officials believed that more than one person had been involved.

On February 23, 1960, for reasons never explained, twenty-three-year-old Horst Otto walked into the police station and confessed to the murder of Manuela, which had taken place six months earlier. He was arrested and charged with the murder, and although he quickly withdrew his confession, he was convicted and served eight years in prison before being released.

Around 1960, Kroll went to work as a toilet attendant, and, afterward, moved to 24 Friesen Street, Laar, in Duisburg, working for Thyssen Industries. He would remain here until his arrest many years later, although he was warned by the landlord that he would be kicked out if he were ever seen attempting to bring young girls into his quarters, as he had on two occasions.

In 1962, Barbara Bruder vanished. Years later, Kroll would confess that he killed the twelve-year-old, but due to a lack of convincing evidence, he was never convicted. Kroll said that, like the others, he had strangled and raped her. She was on her way to a playground in Lützenkirchen, but she never arrived. Her body has never been found.

Petra Giese was killed on Easter Monday, April 23, 1962, in a forest, north of Duisburg. The thirteen-year-old was strangled and raped, her body found among the bushes. She had been visiting a carnival with a friend, and she had become separated from her friend. It is a distinct possibility that Kroll led her away. Her body was found the next day by a search party. She was missing both buttocks, as well as her left arm.

Fifty-two-year-old Vinzenze Kuehn, a single man who worked as a miner, was arrested for her murder. There was sufficient evidence to suspect Kuehn. For one thing, the vehicle he owned, a cross between an automobile and a motorcycle, called a Goggo Isar, was similar to one a farmer claimed to have seen the day of the murder, near the spot where the body was found. Upon checking motor vehicle records, police discovered that only five hundred twenty-two of these vehicles were owned in the area. Of that number, all of the vehicle owners had alibis that were verified and their whereabouts at the time were accounted for—all except for Vinzenze Kuehn.

Secondly, Kuehn had a criminal record, one that made him seem a likely suspect for the type of crime with which he stood accused. Kuehn was a convicted sex offender, more accurately, a child molester. Kuehn was very fond of little girls and had developed a method he used repeatedly.

He waited on them in parks and places that provided access to young girls, who, at that time, were often allowed to go about without parental supervision. At times enticing them with candy, and if that did not work, offering them money, he coerced them into removing their panties and allowing him to give them lessons in masturbation. He followed this up by masturbating himself.

Very few girls ever came forward to accuse Kuehn of inappropriate acts with them, but police always believed the number was far greater than they knew.

There was another reason to believe Petra's death had not been at the hands of Kuehn—he was never known to approach a teenager. Perhaps it was because he was not physically attracted to the womanly attributes of the female form, or simply because he feared older girls were more likely to betray him to their parents and the authorities.

The police, however, were not willing to dismiss the fact that Kuehn owned a Goggo like the one the witness testified to seeing and the fact he had no alibi for the time of the murder. Medical professionals were consulted for their opinion, and the experts stated their belief that any man who engaged in the type of perverse behavior with young girls, which Kuehn admitted to, could potentially "get carried away and end up a rapist and murderer." They theorized that Kuehn had lost control of himself, raped Petra, and upon realizing what he had done, then attempted to cover up his actions by murdering and mutilating her to make law enforcement believe these were the actions of a sadistic sex murderer.

The official postmortem report, which showed Petra had been murdered first and then raped, was ignored, and Vinzenze Kuehn was charged with the rape, murder, and mutilation of Petra Giese. Faced with no evidence he had committed the crime, the jury still found him guilty. Whether their opinion was that the possibility of his guilt existed, or merely that if he was not guilty this time, it was reasonable to believe he was capable of such crimes in the future, the jury voted unanimously to have him put away.

Kuehn was sentenced to twelve years in prison, along with a regimen of psychiatric treatments designed to "rid him of his unnatural interest in little girls and convert him into a useful member of society." Kuehn's psychiatric treatments ended when he was released from prison six years later, having served only half his sentence.

Police at the time believed he continued his pursuit of young girls after his release, but they never found irrefutable proof of this, and no victims ever came forward. Ironically, if Vinzenze Kuehn had not been in police custody at the time, it is likely he would have also been blamed for the rape and murder of another of Joachim Kroll's victims

On June 4, 1962, twelve-year-old Monika Tafel was murdered just outside her hometown of Walsum. She was killed in much the same way as Petra Giese and those before her. Monika's body was discovered seven days later, on June 11, by a police helicopter. Her body had not been hidden but was merely lying in a part of the forest search parties on foot had not gone over.

Monika had been strangled to death before being stripped naked, raped, and masturbated over. As with prior victims, parts of her flesh had been stripped away. Had the local authorities been in contact with the Duisburg police department, perhaps the similarities in the murders of Petra and Monika would have been noticed and Vinzenze Kuehn would have been spared six years in prison, but that did not happen.

Authorities already had a suspect for Monika's murder. Thirty-four-year-old steelworker Walter Quicker, who was known for having an interest in little girls, was taken in as a suspect by police after witnesses came forward to say they had seen him in the company of a young girl on the day of Monika's murder. Quicker vehemently denied the allegations, but authorities produced information showing Quicker was known in the community for having an interest in young girls, and that some of his actions in the past had made his fellow townspeople suspicious of him.

Quicker admitted he was fond of girls, but insisted his fondness was not of a sexual nature. He had always wanted a daughter, he told the police, but he and his wife were unable to have one. Thus, he lavished attention on little girls. Police questioned dozens of young girls in Walsum, and all denied that Walter Quicker had ever behaved inappropriately with them. Not one single child had a bad word to say about Quicker.

This ruined the case against him for the police, who believed Quicker was guilty but were forced to release him from custody. This, however, did not stop the townspeople from persecuting him and deciding to would punish him since law enforcement had not. His wife divorced him on the grounds that she could not stand the disgrace of "being married to a child molester."

People began to jeer and spit at him on the street, and shopkeepers refused to serve him. When he left his house, youngsters would run behind him and ask how many little girls he had raped that day. The town's older residents would howl with laughter. On October 5, 1962, just five months after Monika Tafel's murder, Walter Quicker walked into the forest with a clothesline and hung himself near the very same spot Monika's body had been found, once again causing police and citizens to falsely believe they had found the guilty party.

The actual murderer, Joachim Kroll, was still free, and now also guilty of causing the deaths of two men, as well as the false imprisonment of others. It is regarded as doubtful that Kroll, after discovering how much pleasure he could derive from the crimes, would have gone three years without killing, but upon his arrest, he would state after murdering Monika, the next murder he could remember was not until 1965. There were just too many killings and too much time had passed, he would tell the police. He could remember the murder in 1965, he said, because that was the only man he had killed—and only because he had gotten in the way.

In August of 1965, Hermann Schmitz and his eighteen-year-old fiancé, Marion Veen, were at lover's lane in Grossenbaum, just south of Duisburg. The area had originally been a large rock quarry, but after the pit was no longer needed, it had been filled with water and formed an artificial lake. It was there, along the shore of the lake, under an autumn moon, that the two lovers' destiny would be decided for them.

Kroll had left his apartment that Sunday night around six and arrived by tram in Grossenbaum approximately three hours later. Kroll had exited the tram and was busying himself following women and girls along the streets of the town, hoping for an opportunity to present itself. When none did, he happened to remember the gravel-pit lake, having lived in the area previously for a short time.

He was also aware of what took place at the lake, having often indulged his voyeuristic side by masturbating outside cars, while occupants inside made love, unaware they were being watched. On this occasion, Kroll had worked himself up into such a frenzy that mere masturbation would not do. When he observed the twenty-five-year-old and his fiancé, Kroll made the decision to rape Marion.

The two were passionately making out on the front seat. Little did they know, Kroll had been prowling the area, watching other couples, and by the time he stumbled upon the two of them, he was already formulating a plan to pull off his next crime. What Kroll wanted was Marion, but he needed to do something about Hermann first. He had to find a way to eliminate him from the equation. Thinking he could perhaps get Hermann to leave the car, he used his pocket knife to stab the right front tire, hoping that by the time Hermann started the car, the air would have leaked out, and Kroll would be able to get to Marion while her fiancé was busy with the flat tire.

However, his plan was almost spoiled when Hermann, although apparently realizing the car had a flat tire, instead unexpectedly began to drive away. Had Hermann been more familiar with the area, as Kroll was, his life might have been spared.

Unfortunately, Hermann missed his turn and drove directly into a dead-end road less than a hundred yards from where he had been parked. Arriving at the dead end and realizing the mistake he had made, he turned the car around and started to head back, which allowed Kroll a second chance. When Hermann turned his car around, Kroll was standing in the road, attempting to flag him down.

Hermann was not intimidated by the site of the scruffy little man with shabby clothes and unshaven face. Hermann towered over him with his large athletic build, Kroll's diminutive stature bringing him barely to the youth's shoulder. Believing the man might need assistance, and sensing no danger, Hermann got out of the car to see what the matter was.

Marion, watching through the windshield as her fiancé approached the stranger, saw the two men seeming to exchange a few words, then she suddenly saw something bright and metallic flash in the stranger's hand. As soon as Hermann got within reach, Kroll stabbed him several times. Her eyes wide with terror, Marion watched the love of her life being stabbed repeatedly as the blood flew from the knife's sharp surface in long darts of crimson.

Kroll, feeling that everything was going according to plan, focused his attention on Marion. Using her quick-thinking skills and keeping a cool head, Marion, jumped into the driver's seat and drove full-speed at Kroll, who barely managed to jump out of the way in time, landing in some bushes. Marion, in hopes of either alerting someone or keeping Kroll at bay, then jammed a hairclip into the car horn, which allowed it to blare continuously. Kroll had no desire to pursue a victim who fought back and fled into the darkness on foot. Marion leaped from the car and rushed over to Hermann, who lay surrounded by a pool of his own blood.

The postmortem later showed the first stab had pierced his heart. He was still alive, though just barely, as Marion sank to her knees beside him on the dirt road and gently lifted his head onto her lap. Struggling in his last fleeting moments of life to speak to the woman he adored, all that ushered forth from his mouth was a final gasp. When the first couple to respond to the blaring car horn arrived, they found Marion, the front of her dress saturated with blood, cradling Hermann's lifeless body. Hermann Schmitz was Kroll's only—intentional—male victim.

Grossenbaum was a part of the Duisburg police district, and they quickly responded to the scene. Unfortunately, they had few clues to go on. Marion's description of the assailant was a bit sketchy because she had only seen his face briefly in the headlights. They were able to collect casts of the shape of the knife from the wounds in Hermann Schmitz's chest, but until they had a knife to compare them with, they would do the investigators little good.

Police brought in several men known to frequent lover's lane and spy on couples, but none of the men corresponded with Marion's description, and when questioned, none panned out as possible suspects. Not knowing the possible motive for the murder, police theorized that perhaps it was perpetrated by a jealous ex-lover of either Hermann or Marion. Friends of the couple were brought in and were also questioned about anyone who might have had reason to want Hermann dead, but none of the friends could offer any assistance. The case made its way to the cold case files, and as no one was aware that Marion had been the target, it was not investigated as a sex crime, and it was not associated with Joachim Kroll or any of his previous crimes.

Kroll's next known crime occurred on a Tuesday afternoon, September 13, 1966. Getting off from work, he boarded a train and traveled to the town of Marl, approximately forty miles north of Duisburg, where he immediately began his usual routine of prowling the streets in pursuit of a victim. By seven o'clock, having found no one he deemed suitable, he went to a local park, where he hid in the gathering darkness. As time passed, he became so aroused that he decided the next female who passed by, regardless of age or looks, he would take.

Twenty-year-old Ursula Rohling had just left the Capri Ice Cream Parlour, where she had passed the time with her fiancé, twenty-seven-year-old Adolf Schickel. They had spent the last hour and a half discussing their upcoming nuptials, but as it grew dark, Ursula needed to head home, and the shortest route would take her through Foersterbusch Park and right into the waiting arms of Joachim Kroll.

Kroll's statement to police after he was captured was as follows:

"I saw this woman in the park. She was young, with short hair. I spoke to her. Then I grabbed her around the neck with my right arm and dragged her into the bushes. I threw her on the ground on her back and choked her."

Asked why he had to choke her to death, Kroll replied:

"She could have fought me. Then I couldn't have done it [raped her]. Anyway, she could have told it was me. I choked her until she stopped moving. Then I took off her pants and other things and I did it to her. I left her lying

there and took the train back to Duisburg. When I got home, I was still hot [aroused] and I had it with the doll and did it with my hand a couple of times."

An odd attribute of Kroll's was that unlike many serial killers, he was not interested in his victims once he was done with them, nor the media coverage, or investigation of the murders. One reason why it was difficult for Kroll to remember all of his crimes was because he had taken so little interest in the victims. He rarely knew their name and seemed to have little or no fear police would one day learn his.

If Kroll had checked the newspapers the next day, he would have found that nothing was reported about the death of Ursula Rohling. Ursula was not even initially reported as missing. Her parents, upon realizing their daughter had not returned home from her meeting with Adolf Schickel, first called him, and then the police. Her body was found two days later by a park employee.

Adolf Schickel, although no possible motive could be found, was nevertheless suspected of her murder and taken into custody. He was held under continuous interrogation for three weeks, but his story never wavered. After their meeting, she had set off for home alone, and although he questioned himself if she would not have been killed had he accompanied her home, he stated emphatically that he did not kill her. For three long weeks, he repeated the same phrases, "Why would I kill Ursula? I loved her. We were going to get married. Why would I do such a thing?"

The police answered, "For sex. She refused to let you have sex with her until you were married, so you raped her and killed her." These accusations ignored the facts of the case. The postmortem had concluded that Ursula had been raped after she was killed, and friends informed police that Ursula and Adolf were already known to have had sexual relations, often spending the night together. Despite all this information, police still believed Adolf had murdered his fiancé, and only released him from custody once they realized they had no evidence and legal grounds that would allow them to hold him any longer.

Like Walter Quicker before him, Adolf Schickel had to deal with police and townspeople alike, believing he was guilty of murder. Adolf was also persecuted and ostracized, eventually being chased out of Marl. On January 4, 1967, depressed by Ursula's death and the accusations against him, Adolf drowned himself in the river, just four months after Ursula's murder.

Joachim Kroll, who thought he had only killed one man, was now responsible—with a little help from police and the citizens of Marl—for the death of a third man.

Ilona Harke, a five-year-old girl, was the test subject for a spur-of-the-moment curiosity Kroll had: he wondered what it would be like to drown someone. So, he abducted the little girl in Essen, perhaps winning her over with candy or a doll, the same way he had won over his neighbors' daughters and took her on a train to Wuppertal. There, he drowned little Ilona. Afterward, he raped her body, then cut the flesh from her shoulders and buttocks and took them home to eat. She was found on December 22, 1966.

As with the case in which Kroll failed to kill Marion Veen, he experienced failure once more, in 1967. This time, it was a ten-year-old girl named Gabriele Puettmann that Kroll had set his sights on. She had already known Kroll, or as she knew him, "Uncle Joachim." She lived in the town of Grafenhausen, and Kroll lived in the nearby town of Grafenwald. It was a Thursday when Kroll decided to target Gabriele, in the country that lies between their two towns. Kroll had taken sick leave from work, and Gabriele had just gotten done with her day's classes.

Usually, when young girls went on walks with Uncle Joachim, they came home safely to their parents, though usually full of ice cream or candy. Kroll exercised extreme caution in who he preyed upon and when, so it is very likely that if a girl's family knew he had gone on a walk with them, he would fall under their suspicion if anything were to happen to their daughter. This mild afternoon in June, however, Kroll must have either cast these worries aside or assumed that nobody knew he had gone on a walk with Gabriele.

During their stroll along the road leading from Grafenhausen to Grafenwald, they reached a point where nobody was in sight around them. Kroll knew it was safe to act upon his urges then. He took Gabriele by the hand and led her to a nearby field of wheat, telling her he had something to show her.

Once they were away from the road, Kroll produced a collection of pornographic cartoon booklets. Gabriele was puzzled at first, but it slowly sunk in what the people in these cartoons were doing. She was then overcome by horrible embarrassment and threw her hands up over her eyes. Then, she felt Kroll's hand on her shoulder. Gabriele was not at all frightened by the man's actions at the time, nor did she then believe he would hurt her in any way, but she was indeed embarrassed, ashamed, and rather taken aback, so she promptly ran away. She ran as fast as possible and, ever cautious, Kroll made no attempt to chase after her. Gabriele didn't stop running until she arrived home, and she never went near "Uncle Joachim" again. Still mortified by the incident, she never told anyone about what had happened. It was only when Joachim Kroll was exposed years later as a murderer that she told her story, and undoubtedly felt lucky she had escaped his clutches.

Sixty-one-year-old Maria Hettgen was not nearly as lucky, however. She was killed on July 12, 1969. When a knock came at her door, she opened it, only to find Kroll standing there. Like the others, she was strangled and raped. Although she was a plump woman, Kroll did not remove any of her flesh. Her body was found in her front hall.

On May 19, 1970, thirteen-year-old, Jutta Rahn, was attacked by Kroll on her way home from school on a rainy Thursday afternoon. Jutta lived in a town near Grossenbaum, where Hermann Schmitz had been stabbed and killed. Kroll spotted her at the railway station and followed her into the woods. Grabbing the young girl and dragging her deeper into the forest, he strangled her to death, removed her clothing, and raped her dead body, then masturbated over it. Suddenly, Kroll was struck by the odd feeling that perhaps the girl was not dead after all, and tying her red bra tightly around her neck, choked her again until he was certain she was dead.

Jutta's father and neighbors searched for six hours after she failed to return home from school. Her father found her nude, lifeless corpse where her killer had left it. Another innocent man was to be charged with a murder that Kroll committed. Peter Schay was arrested for her murder. The only evidence against him was that his blood type matched that of the killer, and, due to no other evidence than that, no charges were brought against him. He was taunted around town with cries of "murderer."

His family, additionally, was referred to as the "Murder Gang." The harassment did not stop until Kroll confessed to the murder in 1976.

For the next six years, Kroll stated he did not commit any more murders. The police, however, did not buy it. After all, six years is quite a long time for a man to go without relieving his sexual urges, whether they are normal or sadistic. Law enforcement had a list of fifteen unsolved sex murders from the Ruhr district, most of which were children, they thought Kroll had likely committed. After all, Kroll would later admit to having a poor memory and state that there might have been more or less victims than he remembered.

However, Kroll adamantly insisted he went clean for those six years and got by with only masturbation and his treasured sex doll.

Nevertheless, on May 8, 1976, Karin Toepfer, a ten-year-old, was killed while on her way to school. She was strangled and raped. Kroll admitted to this murder, but he would not be convicted due to a lack of convincing details.

Kroll's repeated evasion of capture would come to a halt on July 3, 1976. Four-year-old Marion Ketter went missing. It was a hot afternoon, and the blonde child had been wearing nothing but panties due to the heat. Suddenly, she vanished from the apartment building on 24 Friesen Street in Laar, where Joachim Kroll lived. The little girl had lived just a few doors down from Kroll, and she had been to a nearby playground that day.

Mrs. Ketter realized at about four in the afternoon that Marion was missing. She searched the area and spoke with some of the other children who were out playing. Then, she called the police, who also spoke with the children. Police then went door-to-door. They had dropped by Kroll's apartment, but everything had appeared to be in order.

That same day, a tenant of Kroll's apartment building, Oscar Muller, went to use the shared bathroom of the building. As he went up the stairs, he ran into Kroll, who was coming down them. "I would not use the toilet if I were you," Kroll advised. "It's all stopped up." When Oscar asked him what was stopping it up, Kroll simply replied, "Guts." After this chilling exchange, Kroll simply disappeared into his apartment.

Oscar, shrugging it off, decided to go and see what was actually wrong with the toilet. He had not taken Kroll's statement very seriously and considered it to be some kind of twisted joke. But, when he approached the toilet, he found what looked to be flesh in the bowl and the water tinted crimson with blood. The color draining from his face; he immediately rushed outside to the street. He approached the nearest policeman and told him of his discovery.

Making their way to the lavatory, the policemen wrenched the porcelain bowl from its mount and dumped the contents into a bucket. There, staring back at them in all their horrendous splendor, were small lungs, kidneys, a liver, and a heart, along with some flesh. The police made their way back to Kroll's apartment and beat loudly at the door. When they entered, they found what still remained of Marion's body chopped up on the kitchen table and a stew simmering on the stove, with what appeared to be its key ingredient—a tiny hand—floating amidst the vegetables. Upon closer inspection, they found that the sink was clogged with entrails, and in the refrigerator, there were portions of the little girl's flesh on several plates, as though they were pre-planned meals. In the freezer, they found more body parts.

Joachim Kroll was arrested and went along quite willingly and without protest. He believed he would receive some sort of surgical procedure that would stay his bloodthirsty desires and make him normal. Due to this belief, after about a day, he confessed to a total of fourteen murders to the police, though he said there might have been more or less because he couldn't remember clearly. He also explained that his murderous desires started when, as a teenager, he saw pigs being slaughtered, and was aroused by the blood.

Coincidentally, Ed Gein gave this same reasoning for his desire to kill. Kroll also admitted that he couldn't maintain an erection with a woman—at least, not when she was conscious—which was why he took to raping his victims. He also confessed he had tried human flesh "on a whim" and liked it. He began to choose victims he thought looked "tasty" and would yield tender flesh. He also stuck with cannibalism to save money on groceries, due to the price of meat being so high.

He went on to speak of how he would come home from committing a murder and, still aroused from his acts, he would have sex with and masturbate over his rubber doll, strangling it while doing so, reenacting his crimes. It also helped him to practice strangulation holds. The pretty, child-sized dolls he used to entice little girls were also used for this purpose. Kroll did not know any of his victims' names, but he could remember the time and place where he had committed a murder.

When shown a picture of a girl, he usually recognized her but hadn't kept up with news reports following his crimes. Often, as the police were taking him to the scene of one of his crimes, they would pass an area where Kroll would stop and announce he had killed someone in that spot. The police would check their files of unsolved murders and, without varying, Kroll was right.

Typically, we make the assumption that a serial killer who got away with murder for twenty years has to have a moderately high IQ. Usually, killers with an extremely low IQ must work alongside an accomplice, who helps them cover their tracks. The mentally handicapped offender is classified by being someone who has difficulty answering questions, limited vocabulary, acts impulsively, limited ability to recall events, prefers young children as friends, and incapable of understanding consequences. This seemed to describe Joachim Kroll very well.

One of the ways Kroll avoided detection was that he sometimes changed the method he used to kill his victims, ranging from stabbing to strangulation to drowning, and he did not always cannibalize his victims. He also killed in many different towns, mostly those which surrounded his own. If he had not killed a child who lived just a few doors down that last time, he likely would have continued getting away with that murder as well.

Because of his tendency to kill in many different areas, and because there were other killers working in the same area as Kroll at the time of the murders, law enforcement thought his work was that of several other people. One of the other reasons Kroll was able to evade capture for two decades was due to the irregular spacing of his crimes, once going six years without committing a murder, though sometimes killing again in the span of a couple of months.

Joachim Kroll was an enigma. He evoked pity in those around him: whether it be his neighbors who saw him as a lonely, simple-minded man who loved their children and only wanted a family of his own or heard his desires to have that simple operation he thought existed and would rid him of his horrendous desires. At the same time, however, he induced horror, terror, and rage.

Upon looking into the eyes of the pictures of his victims, most especially the young girls, one wonders what sort of monster it takes to so brutally take away their lives, for nothing more than a moment's twisted pleasure and a meal made from their remains.

What snapped inside him that cold day of his mother's death? We may never know.

All we can be sure of is Joachim Kroll left a region in terror with a string of bodies and a horde of bloody meals in his wake.

II
Alfred Packer

ALFRED PACKER HAS, OVER THE COURSE OF almost one hundred fifty years, become more legend than man. Stranded on an expedition on the path to find gold, he and five other men were forced to endure a cruel, bitter winter in the mountains of Colorado. Only one man came out of the mountains alive: Alfred Packer, who looked far too fit and healthy for the conditions he had endured.

Packer claimed the other men had died along the way, one after another, and he had killed the last man in self-defense. But how had Packer survived the wilderness? He stated that the men had run out of provisions, but yet, he refused a meal when he came out of the forest. Only later were the corpses of the five men found, all at one campsite.

Alfred Packer would eventually tell a story of suffering and strife and confess to cannibalism. But, did he kill the other men in cold blood, then feast on their flesh, or did he shoot one man in self-defense and only eat his companions to survive? The tale has long since captured the imaginations of many and has become almost like local folklore.

Alfred Packer's story has become more legend and myth, and the historical crime element has been nearly obscured. The case is most certainly a notorious whodunit, stumping even modern forensic experts. Nevertheless, the area of Colorado known as Cannibal Plateau will forever be remembered as the grisly campsite of the "Colorado Cannibal."

Alfred Griner Packer was born November 21, 1842—although he claimed, as do some sources, it was January 21—to parents James and Esther. Some sources spell his name as "Alferd," which is a misspelling either caused by Packer's own inability to spell or, as a more colorful story goes, the way a tattoo artist spelled Packer's name when tattooing it on the man's arm.

From an early age, he suffered from epilepsy. He became a shoemaker in his teens, and, when the Civil War began, he was quick to enlist in Minnesota in Company F, 16th U.S. Infantry Regiment. Due to his epilepsy, he was quickly given an honorable discharge, but that did not stop the lanky, blue-eyed young Alfred. He moved and enlisted in Iowa in Company L, 8th Iowa Cavalry Regiment. Once more, he was honorably discharged due to his illness.

He had also been caught rummaging through dead soldiers' pockets when he worked for an ambulance crew, something that would be echoed later in his life. He then moved on to work in many various fields: mining, trapping, guiding, and hunting. All employments seemed to end when Packer would have an episode caused by his epilepsy.

By 1872, Packer had found his way to Colorado, where he worked again as a miner. In an accident with a sledgehammer, he lost his left pinky and index fingers. Next, he made his way to Utah, working in the mines once more. While Packer was there, news came that there had been gold struck back in Colorado.

A group of men formed to make their way to Colorado to hunt for gold. One of the men in the group, Preston Nutter, described

Packer as "sulky, obstinate, and quarrelsome. He was a petty thief willing to take things that did not belong to him, whether of any value or not." This description of Packer would also be related by others in the future. The group soon grew to twenty-one men, including Packer, who claimed he was the guide.

In November 1873, Alfred Packer and his group left Utah for Colorado gold country. Packer was generally disliked among the men. Not only did he have a tendency to whine and get into arguments, but his epileptic seizures also bothered the other men. The seizures were relatively frequent after the men had set out on their journey. Once, during a seizure, he fell into the campfire and upended a pot of scalding-hot coffee on his face.

Alfred's attitude and epilepsy would turn out to be the least of the group's concerns. They quickly began to grow short on food supplies. In desperation, they found themselves eating horse feed. By January, they had made it into the Ute Indian camp of Chief Ouray, near Montrose, Colorado.

The Ute cared for the enfeebled men and provided them with food and shelter. Chief Ouray urged them to stay at the camp until spring, expressing how dangerous the mountains were and how severe the winters could be. He told them it was forty miles to the nearest Indian reservation. However, it was later revealed the chief had been mistaken. It was, in fact, seventy-five miles.

A handful of the men decided to ignore Chief Ouray's advice, not wanting to be beaten to the gold they had come all this way in search of. They believed they could take some provisions and easily make it the forty miles in no time.

The men were Alfred Packer, Shannon Bell, Frank Miller, George "California" Noon, James Humphrey, and Israel Swan. Packer himself claimed another group set out before them, but there is not much evidence to support those claims, nor is there any evidence to support his statement he was the leader of the original group.

The rest of the original group eventually made it to the Indian reservation 75 miles away. However, weeks passed and there was no sign of Packer's party. It looked bleak for the six men. Finally, on April 16, 1874, Alfred Packer appeared, alone, at the Los Pinos Indian Agency. He was oddly fit for having spent two months stranded in heavy snow and trekking through the wilderness with little food.

When one of the original twenty men asked him where the rest of his party was, Packer claimed he had been left behind by the rest of the men and had somehow managed to find his way to the agency. He thought they would have beaten him there. He also refused the offer of a meal, which was rather questionable, since he claimed to have survived off rosebuds and rabbits.

Suspicions began to rise when it was noticed that Packer had in his possession a skinning knife belonging to Frank Miller. Packer left for Saguache, Colorado, alongside a few of the men from the original party, where he ended up spending a suspicious amount of money. This, along with all the other odd occurrences, raised doubts among the men from the original party. Packer was brought in for questioning by General Adams of the Los Pinos Indian Agency. He confessed a darker story, one of many versions of confessions he would tell for years to come.

Packer claimed that bad weather had immediately put the party in danger, with a terrible storm coming a few days after they had left Chief Ouray's camp. He said they'd only had a week's worth of food rations for every man. Due to the extreme weather conditions, "Old Man Swan" had died and was then eaten by the other men. Four or five days afterward, he alleged, James Humphrey died and was also eaten. Packer had found Humphrey's wallet on his body and taken it, stating it had one hundred and thirty-three dollars in it. Sometime later, Packer was carrying wood and, upon returning to the campsite, found that Frank Miller had been killed, and the other two men told him it was by accident. He, too, was eaten. Then, Packer states, Bell shot "California" with Israel Swan's gun and attempted to kill Packer, who shot him in return.

General Adams decided to ask Packer to accompany a search party in an effort to find the men's bodies. He knew that the evidence found would either prove or disprove Packer's testimony. Packer led the party but claimed he couldn't remember exactly where the campsite was since it had all been covered in snow. Later, he would allege a different reason for not leading the search party to the campsite. Regardless, the circumstances were too suspicious, and Packer was arrested and jailed just outside of Saguache. The jail was a small building, little more than a log cabin. However, just a few months later, in August, someone slipped Packer a makeshift key to unlock his leg irons. He escaped and vanished without a trace.

Coincidentally, on the same day Packer escaped, the bodies of the five men were found. All were found at one campsite, not strewn out along the way as Packer had described. They appeared to have been killed in their sleep. There are different stories as to who found the bodies, but the only one with any evidence to support it was

John A. Randolph, an artist for Harper's Weekly Magazine, stumbled across the corpses at Slumgullion Pass.

Besides looking as if they had been killed in their sleep, the men's feet were bound in blankets and they had no shoes near them. Also missing were guns and other items one would have expected to find. Even more disturbing was that one of the men appeared to be missing his head. Knowing these had to be the missing prospectors, Randolph immediately set to sketching them. Afterward, he reported his findings to the authorities. One of the men from Packer's original party, Preston Nutter, positively identified the remains as those of Packer's companions. Through a process of elimination, they discovered that the headless body belonged to Frank Miller.

Packer remained at large for nearly nine years. One day, while in Wyoming, one of the members of the original prospecting party, Jean "Frenchy" Cabazon encountered a man going by the name of John Schwartze. Immediately, he recognized the voice as being that of Alfred Packer. He reported Packer to the local sheriff, who arrested the man and contacted General Adams. Once apprehended, Packer decided to make a second confession. His story changed yet again.

Packer said they had gone over the main range and camped near a lake twice; the second time, directly above the lake. The next morning, they cut holes in the ice on the lake and attempted to fish but did not catch anything. They crossed the lake and went into a timber grove, and Packer said that all the men were crying, and one was angry. Then, Israel Swan asked Packer if he could go up and see if he could see anything from the mountains, so Packer took his gun and went. He said he couldn't see anything but snow. He was gone nearly the full day, and once he returned, he found Shannon Bell, who he said had "acted crazy" that morning, sitting in front of a fire, roasting a piece of meat he had cut from Frank Miller. His body was lying the furthest from the fire, while the other men's bodies were lying near the fire.

Packer said that Miller's head had been crushed in with the hatchet, and the other men had cuts on their foreheads from the same weapon. As Packer neared the fire, Shannon Bell jumped up and came toward him with the hatchet, so Packer shot him once in the belly. Once the hatchet fell forward, Packer picked it up and hit Bell in the head with it. He said he camped by the fire that night but did not sleep.

The next day, he attempted to follow his tracks back up the mountain, but the snow was too deep, so he returned and went into the pine timbers and fashioned a shelter out of two sticks covered in pine boughs. The shelter, about three feet high, was where he stayed until he was finally able to make it out of the mountains. Then, he went to the campsite and covered the men up, took the piece of meat that Shannon Bell had allegedly been cooking. Next, he said, he made a new fire near his own camp and cooked the piece of meat and ate it.

He expressed that he attempted every day to make it out of the mountains, but he was unable. He continued to live off the flesh of the men the sixty days or so he was trapped there. When the snow began to have a crust, he followed the creek until he found a place where a big slide of yellowish clay seemed to come down the mountain. He started to go up, but his feet got wet and froze the soles under his toes, due to the fact that he only had blankets wrapped around them. He camped before he reached the top of the hill and made himself a fire, where he cooked some of his fallen companions' flesh and carried it with him for food, along with one blanket.

He alleged there were seventy dollars amongst the men, so he took it, along with one gun. He said Shannon Bell had a fifty-dollar bill in his pocket and all the others had twenty dollars combined. Packer himself had twenty dollars. He added that if there was any more money among the men, he did not know of it and it remained there. He had cooked the men's flesh and carried it with him in a bag, but only ate a little at a time, and had eaten the last of it at his final campsite before he arrived at the Los Pinos Indian Agency.

Packer also claimed that when he led the search party to find the men, they came to the mountains overlooking the stream where all the men had died, but he did not want to go any further. He did not want to go back to the campsite himself. He said that he would have taken General Adams to the campsite if he had stood there a little longer, but "they" told him to go away, although he refused to say who among the search party "they" were. He also informed General Adams of how he had escaped from the jail outside of Saguache—with a key fashioned from a penknife blade. Once he had escaped, he went to Arkansas and worked for a man named John Gill, eighteen miles below Pueblo, then rented Gilbert's ranch further south, put in a crop of corn, sold it to Gill, then went to Arizona.

Alfred Packer's trial began on April 6, 1883. He was only tried for the murder of Israel Swan, whose remains were said to have shown evidence of an intense struggle, which made Packer seem far more violent than he had claimed to be. Packer was tried in Lake

City, a town that had just been established, with Judge Gerry Melville presiding. Packer pled not guilty.

Preston Nutter, who had identified the men's bodies when they had been discovered, testified as to what he had seen that day. Using illustrations, he showed the jury how the men's bodies had been positioned, then described their wounds. He said that every man had wounds from a hatchet on their heads, except one, whose head he said was "mashed in." The coroner did not testify, nor had he even made a written report of what he had found in the first place.

Packer took the stand and, over the course of two hours, told several glaring lies, such as his age, the fact he had enlisted in the army twice and been discharged both times, his exact military service, and the cause of his epilepsy—which he claimed had been caused during walking guard duty. Once more, he claimed he had only killed Shannon Bell, and it had been in self-defense. Then, his story seemed to revert to its original state. He claimed the men who had survived longer than the others had eaten each other. During these events, he was away scouting for food. When he returned, human flesh was already being cooked over the fire. However, in another deviation of his story, he said he had only eaten the meat from two bones, which belonged to Bell and Miller.

As if the fact that his story was still evolving and changing with each retelling was not bad enough, Packer also became superficial and argumentative. He also admitted to taking the victims' belongings. None of this made his image any better in the eyes of the jury.

The jury found Packer guilty of the murder of Israel Swan on, ironically, Friday the 13th.

He was sentenced to death.

It has become a popular story that the judge delivered his sentence by saying:

> *"Stand up yah voracious man-eatin' sonofabitch and receive yir sintince. When yah came to Hinsdale County, there was siven dimmycrats. But you, yah et five of 'em, goddam yah. I sintince yah t' be hanged by th' neck ontil yer dead, dead, dead, as a warnin' ag'in reducin' th' Dimmycratic populayshun of this county. Packer, you Republican cannibal, I would sintince ya ta hell, but the statutes forbid it."*

In truth, what the judge said was far more eloquent. He began by stating:

"It becomes my duty as the Judge of this Court to enforce the verdict of the jury rendered in your case and impose on you the judgment which the law fixes as the punishment of the crime you have committed. It is a solemn, painful duty to perform." He went on to describe how horrific the crimes seemed and how, in the beauty of these glorious mountains, such dark deeds had been committed.

Afterward, he stated:

"You and your victims had had a weary march, and when the shadow of the mountains fell upon your little party and night drew her sable curtain around you, your unsuspecting victims lay down on the ground and were soon lost in the sleep of the weary; and when thus sweetly unconscious of danger from any quarter, and particularly from you, their trusted companion; you cruelly and brutally slew them all."

It seems that, though Packer had only been convicted of the murder of Israel Swan, the judge believed he had murdered all five men. The judge ended by saying, *"Packer be hung by the neck until you are dead, dead, dead, and may God have mercy upon your soul."*

A couple of years later, however, Packer won the right to a new trial. He had been tried in 1883 for a crime he had committed in

1874, and there had been no state murder statute in 1874 that allowed for this. He had been arrested when Colorado was a territory, and was tried after Colorado became a state. He was tried for the deaths of all five men, and, instead of murder, the charge was voluntary manslaughter. His trial took place in Gunnison, and he was convicted on all five counts. Packer was sentenced to forty years.

He continued to proclaim his innocence and never stopped pushing to be pardoned.

Packer also wrote to the Denver Post on August 7, 1897. In his writing, he told a third version of the events that took place in the brutal early months of 1874.

This third confession was his longest yet. He began by saying that in the fall of 1873, a party of men left Salt Lake City by wagon. He said they were already deficient in supplies from the very beginning. Their supplies were beginning to dwindle by the time they reached the Green River. He went on to describe they were already feeling the pangs of hunger at this point in their journey. For five days, they had been surviving on horse feed, which was made of chopped barley. At this point, they stumbled on to Chief Ouray's camp and received assistance there. Chief Ouray had told them the mountains were impassible at this time of year, so they camped two miles out of his camp and purchased supplies from them.

After a week of camping in this spot, Packer said a man named Lutzenheiser started for the Los Pinos Indian Agency. They had been told by Chief Ouray that it was only forty miles to the Agency, although it was, in fact, eighty. Lutzenheiser and the four other men that had gone with him had few provisions, only what they carried with them, and they were on foot. The details of Lutzenheiser seems very similar to his own party's story.

He says that, quickly, the men's provisions ran low, so they cast lots to see who would be killed first and subsequently eaten by the other men. Right as they were about to do it, however, they spotted a coyote and killed it to eat it. As the party reached a cattle camp where the town of Gunnison would soon stand, Lutzenheiser shot a cow.

The man in charge of the herd saw the tracks left by Lutzenheiser and, upon following them, found Lutzenheiser in "an exhausted condition." He took Lutzenheiser back to his camp, then followed his trail back and found the remaining four men, which he also took to his camp. The men stayed at the camp until they were in a better condition, at which point they set out for the Los Pinos Indian Agency once more and arrived in an exhausted condition. He added, all this was sworn to at his trial and was a matter of court record.

Packer decided to return to the story of his party. He said there had been two trails to the Agency, and they had taken the upper trail in hopes of reaching the Agency. They were also on foot and carried as many provisions as they were able to in blankets. After nine days, they ran out of provisions. The snow was incredibly deep. In order to travel at all, they had to keep to the top of the divide, which led to the top of the Rocky Mountains. All their matches had been used and they were carrying their fire in an old coffee pot.

Three or four days after running out of food, they took to eating their moccasins, which Packer said were made of rawhide. "Our suffering at this time was most intense. Such, in fact, that the inexperienced cannot imagine." He stated that they couldn't retrace their steps because of how quickly the snow fell and covered them. In places, the snow had been blown away from wild rose bushes, so they gathered the rosebuds, cooked them, and ate them. In following the divides, they soon came to the tip of the Rocky Mountains. Their feet were now wrapped in blankets. They still didn't have anything to kill for food, and there were no longer any rose bushes.

"Starvation had fastened its deathly talons upon us and was slowly but most tortuously driving us into the state of imbecility." He said that Bell had already succumbed to insanity, and the rest of the party was afraid of him, as well as afraid that their inevitable doom was to also end up in such a state.

The group discussed their options and decided to come down off the mountain, especially seeing as they couldn't tell if they had passed the Agency or not, due to the fact that it was constantly either snowing or blowing. They camped one night above the lake and, in the morning, Packer climbed the mountain to see if he could spot any sign of civilization. The snow was deep enough for it to take an entire day to make this trip and return.

As he neared the camp, he saw a horrific sight. He saw no one but Bell and, when he attempted to speak to him, he grabbed a hatchet and, with the "look of a terrible maniac," started for Packer. So, Packer shot him, but the noise of the gunshot didn't rouse any of the rest of the party. Packer ran toward the campfire, where he found his companions dead. "Can you imagine my situation? My companion's dead, and I left alone? I was surrounded by the midnight horrors of starvation as well as those of utter isolation."

He says he saw a piece of flesh cooking over the fire, which Bell had cut from Miller's leg. He took this flesh, laid it aside, and covered the bodies of his companions, then stayed with them through the night. In the morning, he moved one thousand yards below. He stated he distinctly remembered taking a piece of the flesh and cooking it in a tin cup, but, after eating it, became sick and suffered terribly.

Then his mind failed him; he knew he definitely ate some of the flesh, but his mind was a total blank for a period of time. When his mind returned, he discovered, by his tracks, that he had wandered off and found rosebuds, which he had been stewing in his tin cup, by force of habit. He expressed, "The record of time now becomes a nonentity."

He couldn't remember how long he remained here, if it was near the close of the year, or how near spring was. When the weather began to moderate, he wandered once more in search of rosebuds and found himself at the Los Pinos Indian Agency. He was very surprised, especially so, considering that, in his search for food, he had wandered forty miles.

He said he was taken care of for three weeks—which was a lie; he had been in relatively good shape—and that, at the end of these three weeks, the remaining of the twenty-one men from the original party came through with a group of Indians. Packer claims that, when questioned about the whereabouts of the rest of his party, he replied that he had killed Bell, who had apparently killed the others—another lie. He then says that, in a day or two, he went with the teams over to Siwatch, where he remained until General Adams returned from Denver.

He then explained to the General all he knew, and a party was sent out to find the men, but they couldn't continue on, because of the snow—in truth, they continued on just fine, led by Packer, who was still claiming the men had died along the trail, one-by-one. After returning to the Agency, Packer said he was turned over to the sheriff of Siwatch, with whom he remained until the middle of July, when the sheriff asked Packer if he could remember where exactly he had passed through during his expedition. Once Packer gave him as complete an explanation as he could, the sheriff told him to go away and not permit it to worry him.

Packer did as advised and went away, but after ten years, he was arrested and charged with the murder of his companions. He continued on to detail his trials briefly, then ended by going into a long-winded tangent, saying he was, as ever before, a member of the human family, although isolated and away from that which is dear to the heart of any man.

"Am I the villainous wretch which some have asserted me to be? No man can be more heartily sorry for the acts of twenty-four years ago than I. I am more a victim of circumstances than of atrocious designs. No human being living can say that I, in cold blood, with evil intent, murdered my companions upon that awful occasion. What could be the object of my taking their lives in a wanton manner? I bear no malice towards living man. Even though I may feel that I have been unjustly dealt with, still that Supremacy which rules over all knows that I forgive as I would wish to be forgiven."

He went on to express he would have been far better off if his execution had taken place years before, and that then, he could be alongside his fallen companions, whose ghosts, he assured, did not haunt him, because they knew his true innocence. He conveyed the brightness in his future, and his one hope was that he would be allowed the opportunity to show the world he was "less black than had been painted." He thanked the people who had helped him and stated his desire to be given a pardon. He ended the letter with, "Were it not for the flame of hope which burns forever in the human heart, life would certainly be beyond endurance. Gratefully Yours, Alfred Packer."

Newspapers reported his efforts, and a man by the name of Duane Hatch took notice. He had known Packer back in Wyoming and had worked with him on a cattle ranch. Hatch went to visit Packer and discovered he was nothing like the bloodthirsty monster the newspapers made him out to be. Packer often braided horsehair into belts and watch fobs to sell to people who visited the prison. With the money he received, he would buy clothes for prisoners who had been paroled or give them money to pay a month's rent until they could get a job and pay it themselves. It was said he never expected to be repaid for these favors. One prison guard even called Packer "the soul of generosity" and said he didn't care at all for money.

Hatch aided Packer in his relentless pursuit for a pardon, hiring the best lawyers available, and asking every customer who came into his barbershop to sign a petition to free Packer. Thanks to his efforts, the public began to see Packer in a different light, a man who had been forced to survive in the wilderness by eating his fallen companions, who had been convicted of manslaughter on flimsy circumstantial evidence.

Eventually, the efforts began to get somewhere. A reporter for the Denver Post, Polly Pry, began to fight toward Packer's freedom. Prior to her efforts, Packer had already made a petition for parole, but with her help, the help of the Post, and the help of many other people who had begun to view Packer in the light of innocence, they finally got to the Governor. Just before the Governor left office in 1901, he paroled Alfred Packer but did not pardon him.

Packer, agreeing with the Governor not to make a profit off his crimes, went on to become a guard for the Denver Post. He quickly tired of this life and went to work, once more, in mining, although this time, it seems he managed several mines.

In the final years of his life, living in Littleton, he was known to share stories of the Old West with children, amusing them greatly. He died April 24, 1907, of a stroke. He maintained his innocence until the very end. Due to having been in the Civil War, the military paid for his funeral and headstone. His headstone reads, "Alfred Packer, Co. F. 16 U.S. Inf."

On July 17, 1989, the bodies of the five men buried at Cannibal Plateau were exhumed, led by James Starrs, who was a professor of law and forensic science at George Washington

University. Starrs told reporters that his findings showed that Packer was "guilty as sin and his sins were all mortal."

He also stated what they had discovered during the examination of the bones: none of the victims had been shot. Four of the men were struck on the head with a hatchet. The fifth skull, however, was not found. The bones of all five skeletons showed cut marks likely made when the flesh was being cut off, which Starrs said was unmistakable proof of cannibalism.

In 1994, David Bailey, Curator of History at the Museum of Western Colorado, began an investigation into a Colt revolver in the museum that had supposedly been found at the 1874 crime scene. Upon reading about Shannon Bell having been shot, Bailey inspected Bell's bones and discovered what appeared to be a gunshot wound in the pelvis area and that Bell's wallet had a bullet hole in it.

In 2001, lead fragments in the ground under Shannon Bell's remains were positively matched to the bullets in the gun. On the bullet hole, however, James Starrs claimed the hole in Bell's hip was likely caused by a gnawing, foraging animal and not a bullet.

Even though it is still hotly debated as to whether or not Alfred Packer was guilty of murder, it is no debate that he was indeed a cannibal. That much, he admitted to himself. We will never know for certain what took place in the snow-engulfed Colorado mountains in the early months of 1874. The evidence revealed during these recent investigations seems to align quite well with Alfred Packer's final story. However, we will never be sure whether Shannon Bell killed the four men, or if Packer, himself, killed all five.

Perhaps, even Packer was not sure of what happened in those desolate, snowy woods. He may have been entirely delusional from starvation and exposure to the elements. Though the first two stories he told, those of being abandoned by the men and of the men dying off one-by-one, were not truthful, it is possible Packer was so mentally detached from what he had been through that he believed those to be the truth. He may have even believed Shannon Bell had attacked him, as he stated in his second confession, due to his mental state at the time.

With modern-day forensic testing, we are able to figure out those horrible events from that cruel winter much better than they were able one hundred and forty-four years ago, and the bodies of the men have given evidence that corroborates Alfred Packer's story.

Perhaps, Alfred Packer truly is a victim of circumstance, or perhaps, he is a cold-blooded killer who killed five men in the remote wilderness, robbed them, and ate their remains.

Either way, Alfred Packer has gone down in history and will forever be remembered as the "Colorado Cannibal."

III

Boone Helm

THOUGH ONE CAN NEVER BE FULLY CERTAIN whether or not Alfred Packer was a cold-blooded murderer, there is a story of one man who not only cruelly murdered and ate under the same circumstances but killed and ate victims prior to setting foot in the wilderness.

Boone Helm, the "Kentucky Cannibal," was most assuredly a cold-hearted killer with a penchant for cannibalism and a lifelong desire for chaos. The one time he was not chaotic, rampaging, and violent was at his execution. Then, and only then, he was peaceful.

On February 15, 1864, a local newspaper reported:

"Hung at Last - The Notorious Boone Helm, who so long succeeded in escaping the ends of justice, has been lynched..."

Doubtless, there were tears shed by those who learned the cold-blooded killer had finally been dispatched from this world. Having killed untold numbers of men—only eleven victims could be directly attributed to Helm—without remorse, committed cannibalism, and escaped from custody on multiple occasions, the thing perhaps that caused people to cower in fear the most was that Helm was known to be a cannibal.

Under the presumption that any man, upon tasting human flesh, was thereafter unable to fight the urge to kill and eat his fellow man, citizens of the day did not wait for the wheels of justice to rid them of Boone Helm. Instead, they took matters into their own hands.

A newspaper article detailing his last escape from jail, just prior to his death, recounts Helm's admission of cannibalism to the authorities:

"The first clue of the detectives was the report that two men had been seen trudging up the Frazer River on foot. When overtaken, he was so exhausted by fatigue and hunger, that

it would have been impossible for him to have continued many hours longer. Upon being asked what had become of his companion, he replied, 'Why, do you suppose I'm fool enough to starve to death when I can help it? I ate him of course.'"

An arresting officer at the time went on to say that since the companion had neither been seen nor heard from since, and Helms was known to have cannibalized victims in the past, he was inclined to believe the prisoner. Boone Helm's remains lie beneath a metal gravestone, placed there January 14, 1864, by the vigilantes who tried him in secret, and hung him in public, from the cross beam of an uncompleted building in the center of town...

On January 28th, 1827, a son was born to Mr. and Mrs. Joseph Helm in the hills of Lincoln, Kentucky. He was given the name Levi Boone Helm. The large family was respected and hard-working, though, in time, Levi would prove himself to be nothing of the sort. When Levi was a young boy, his family made the move from the Knobs region of Kentucky to Missouri.

Once in his teenage years, Levi quickly acquired the reputation for being an agitator, often provoking fights with other men. His favorite activity seemed to be demonstrating his strength and agility, whether it be by fighting or by throwing his Bowie knife into the ground and retrieving it from atop his horse at full gallop. He grew to resent authority and once rejected a sheriff's attempt to arrest him, instead riding his horse up the front steps of the courthouse into the building while court was in session, then proceeding to give the judge a piece of his mind.

Helm married Lucinda Brown in 1848. The two were young, her being seventeen and Helm being twenty-one. Rather than settling down, Helm kept up his antics and began to show his dark side toward his new wife. Hot-tempered and a raging alcoholic, Helm would often ride his horse into their home, then proceed to beat his wife. The two had a daughter together named Lucy. But the violence topped with Helm's drunken antics brought Lucinda to a breaking point. She divorced him, and Helm's father paid the cost for it.

Helm had succeeded in both bankrupting his father and ruining his family's reputation. When news came in 1850 that there was gold to be found in California, Helm decided to leave for that direction. Needless to say, the community must have been eager to see him go.

Helm's cousin, Littlebury Shoot, was asked to go with Helm to California. He began to rethink those plans about accompanying his cousin when he realized he had a reputation for being quarrelsome and violent. When Shoot let it be known that he was not going across the country with Helm, Helm was offended. In a typical fit of rage, Helm stabbed Shoot in the chest.

Shoot died instantly, and Helm took off, alone, as hastily as possible. He had hoped to be far away by the time anyone discovered what he had done, but relatives and friends of Shoot were on his trail and caught up with him. The group eventually captured him, but his behavior made them quickly realize they were not equipped to deal with him alone. He was handed over to authorities and placed in an insane asylum shortly thereafter.

Once in the asylum, Helm began plotting his escape. He convinced his guard to allow him to take walks in the woods. Helm built up the guard's trust during each walk the two took. Eventually, the walks alongside the guard became routine and Helm felt he fully had the guard's trust. At last, he was able to escape. He tricked the guard and made a break for it.

For a second time, Helm headed for California. On the way, he murdered several more men, usually in confrontations in which he was likely the instigator, but it was also theorized he killed miners to rob them of their gold. This theory holds water, due to the fact that Helm had plenty of money on him, as would be discovered later.

It is unsure exactly how many people Helm killed during this time, but finally, people began to take notice of what he was doing. Helm knew the townsfolk would not merely put him in an asylum. In order to escape vigilante justice and definitely being killed as retribution, Helm and six other men fled to Oregon. It was to these men that Helm confessed he had cannibalized some of his victims. "Many's the poor devil I've killed, at one time or another... and the time has been that I have been obliged to feed on some of 'em."

Just as happened with Alfred Packer, Helm and his companions were confronted by a ferocious winter. After an attack by Native Americans, they were pushed further into the wilderness and became somewhat lost. The men, who were on horseback, had few provisions with them. Eventually, they resorted to killing their horses, eating the meat, and fashioning the skin into snowshoes. One by one, the men began to weaken and had to be left behind to die from exposure and starvation in the frozen wasteland. Near the end of the journey, in which they were still quite a ways from civilization, there were only two men left; Helm and a man named Burton.

The two found an abandoned cabin. Burton was weak and could not go on any further. We have only Helm's claims to go on. Helm went to the nearby Fort Hall, but it, like the cabin, was abandoned for the winter. He returned to begin collecting firewood. He expressed that, as he went about his task, he heard a gunshot. Rushing inside the cabin, he found that Burton had shot himself, preferring to die quickly rather than the slow death he was facing. Helm, who had already confessed to being a cannibal, quickly decided not to let a potential meal go to waste, especially when starving. He subsequently ate one of Burton's legs, then wrapped the other up in a flannel shirt to take with him on his journey to find civilization.

Helm was eventually found at an Indian reservation, similar to Packer, and had $1400 in coins on him. A generous man helped to feed, clothe, and transport Helm to Salt Lake City, but Helm did not offer to repay the man for his trouble, nor even simply thank him.

In Salt Lake City, he became a hitman and eventually wanted by the law. He fled back to California, despite also being infamous there. Once he arrived, a rancher befriended him and took him in, helping him to hide. Helm, for reasons unknown, expressed his gratitude by killing the man. Then, he was back off to Oregon.

In Oregon, Helm killed once more, though this murder enraged the townsfolk. Dutch Fred was a much-beloved man, who had been unarmed and not instigated any confrontation with Helm. Helm shot him, and some believed he did so at the request of an enemy of Fred's, perhaps for hire.

Helm, knowing how greatly he had angered the town, fled once more. By fall, he had made it to British Columbia, far north from where he had started. He was yet again faced with a brutal winter. He was in the company of another fugitive and had learned his lesson on surviving harsh climates from his prior experience. This time, he killed the man himself and survived off his flesh.

Helm was sent back to Oregon by British Columbia authorities. When it came time for his trial for the murder of Dutch Fred, Helm contacted his wealthy brother, "Old Tex." Helm convinced his brother to pay off witnesses who were to testify at his trial. With no witnesses, he was not convicted and released.

Helm followed his brother to Texas, but shortly reappeared at the various settlements he had gone to before. It seems he had not learned anything about returning to the places where he was wanted. He was right back to killing again, moving from place to place after a murder, just as he had done before his arrest.

Helm eventually joined Henry Plummer's gang of highwaymen. Henry Plummer was an outlaw who had been elected sheriff of Bannack, Montana, where he had originally traveled to prospect for gold. However, after he had been elected sheriff, the number of robberies and murders of those transporting goods out of the area increased dramatically.

Helm and four other members of the gang were arrested by the Montana Vigilantes and tried in secret. Helm claimed not to know the reason why he had been brought before the judge and went on to state he had never killed a man in his life. He was made to kiss the Bible, which he then swore over before proceeding to perjure himself. He went on to accuse his fellow gang member and close friend, Jack Gallagher, of crimes which he himself had committed.

A large crowd gathered January 14, 1864, to see the five men hang at the unfinished log cabin, where ropes had been passed over the ridge pole. The front of the structure was fully open, allowing the many spectators to see the hangings in full view. Each criminal stood on a box, which would be kicked out from under him when the time came.

Helm was calm and unfazed, stating he was not afraid to die. He then asked for a glass of whiskey and told Gallagher to "stop making such a fuss." The matter of confessions and last offices of those praying for the criminals was taking longer than expected, and Helm was irritated by the delay. He spat, "For God's sake, if you're going to hang me, I want you to do it and get through with it." As he watched Jack Gallagher be stripped before he was hanged, Helm demanded that Gallagher give him his overcoat.

One of the men jumped from the box he had been standing atop. Helm, perhaps amused, said, "There's one gone to Hell." After Helm's offbeat statement, Jack Gallagher was hanged. Helm watched on coolly as the man struggled, declaring evenly, "Kick away, old fellow. My turn next. I'll be in Hell with you in a minute."

Next came Helm's turn. An embittered Confederate, he stated, "Every man for his principles! Hurrah for Jeff Davis!" He then cried louder, "Let 'er rip!" Then, he leaped from his box. With that, the "Kentucky Cannibal's" lifetime of murder and violence came to an end.

Boone Helm, as made especially apparent by his final moments, saw little value in the lives of either himself or others. He was a man unfazed by, yet hooked on, death. By his words and actions just before his execution, one can easily draw the conclusion he was without guilt or remorse. He was the violent, chaotic sort who did whatever they desire. His life was marked with recklessness and aggression.

It is not uncommon to hear stories of murder from the Old West. It is equally as frequent one hears about people getting lost or stranded in the unforgiving wilderness in Helm's time period and resorting to cannibalism to survive. However, Helm was a ruthless serial killer, and no one has a clue exactly how many victims he claimed. Additionally, he had admitted to being a cannibal before setting foot in the mountains during his first journey and stated he would eat any of the men present if he had to.

According to his own words, he did not only eat human flesh in survival situations. In some circumstances, he killed out of anger, and in some, he likely killed in order to rob the victim. But there are a few cases in which we are not entirely sure of the motive, such as Dutch Fred's case. It is likely that Helm simply enjoyed killing.

It all ended that cold January day, a day as cold as the disposition of the "Kentucky Cannibal."

IV
Tsutomu Miyazaki

D R. MICHAEL STONE, BEST KNOWN FOR A SCALE he developed to measure "gradations of evil," studied the case of Tsutomu Miyazaki, known as the "Otaku Murderer," and his results were surprising.

Stone's scale, patterned after Dante's levels of hell, is comprised of twenty-two levels, beginning with one—Least Evil—and ending with twenty-two—Most Evil.

Ted Bundy, arguably one of the most notorious serial killers and sadistic individuals of all time, was ranked by Dr. Stone as seventeen. Miyazaki, the myopic misanthrope, who spent much of his time immersed in a fantasy world of manga and horror flicks, was ranked just below Bundy as sixteen.

When police searched Miyazaki's room following his arrest, they were amazed to find an extensive collection of VHS tapes, many of a pornographic nature, numbering in the thousands. Many Japanese, already worried by loners such as Miyazaki, who spent most, if not all of their free time watching videos of a sexually violent nature, lobbied for a ban of such materials, fearing more crimes would follow.

When details of Miyazaki's crimes hit the news, The New York Times described them as completely "un-Japanese," but the perpetrator was very much Japanese.

Individuals who refer to themselves as otaku are not necessarily antisocial because they detest society, but because they have a fear of socializing with others. Socializing is primarily confined to computers, with otaku friendships of several years never advancing to a stage where individuals meet in real life: simply no desire to do so.

Several members of the otaku community were outraged at Miyazaki being labeled as "otaku" by the press, stating that because Miyazaki made a conscious choice to leave his home in order to hunt victims, he should not be considered otaku. Otaku only venture out when absolutely necessary, for work or school, and readily admit they do not seek out sexual partners.

Sexually stimulating literature and media are used to masturbate to, and when asked how they will go about producing future generations if no one chooses to copulate, in true otaku fashion, they answer that technology will develop a solution to that problem. "Otaku," or not, Tsutomu Miyazaki was a depraved killer whose twisted desires matched his twisted limbs.

Born August 21, 1962, Tsutomu Miyazaki was a small, premature child with a deformity that would forever cause him to be ostracized. His hands were fused to his wrists, which caused him to have to turn his entire arm just to rotate his hand. His hands also appeared gnarled, deformed, and overall strange-looking.

It came out during his trial that he was not his mother's biological son; in fact, he was the product of an incestuous relationship between his father and his father's sister, which resulted in a pregnancy. Perhaps this explains his deformities, but, regardless, it still caused other children to shy away from him and to bully him once he entered elementary school.

Miyazaki was additionally nervous trying to get to know other children because he realized how disturbed others were by his hands. His insecurity, coupled with the other children's actions towards him, caused him to keep to himself and have no friends. Even his sisters tended to keep away from him, just as repulsed by his birth defect.

He attended high school in Nanako, Tokyo, where he was still cold-shouldered by the other students. Once more, he mostly kept to himself, which allowed him plenty of time to focus on his studies. Subsequently, he was a star student for a while. Then, he began to lose focus. This likely marked the point when he began to immerse himself fully in his fantasy world, losing sight of any aspirations he may have harbored for the real world.

His grades dropped dramatically, and he gave up on his dream to study English and become a teacher. When Miyazaki graduated, he ranked forty out of fifty-six in his class. Because of this low placement, he was not given the customary admission to Meiji University. Instead, he went to a local junior college and studied to become a photo technician.

Miyazaki moved back into his parents' house in the mid-1980s. He shared a room with his oldest sister. His father owned a newspaper company and his family was very important in Itsukaichi, where they lived. Miyazaki's father wanted him to take over the business, but Miyazaki adamantly opposed this. Miyazaki continued to isolate himself. He was a loner not only among his peers, but among his family, as well. His younger sisters were still ashamed of him. Miyazaki struggled with the emotions that came with this and expressed later that he truly desired "being listened to about [his] problems." However, he thought his parents "would not have heard [him]; [he] would have been ignored." He also stated that at this point, he began to contemplate suicide.

Though he felt rejected by his family, Miyazaki found solace in his grandfather. He felt his grandfather truly supported him and felt that he could always go to his grandfather for guidance. However, in May 1988, his grandfather passed away, shattering his world and his already damaged psyche. Miyazaki went so far as to eat his grandfather's ashes after he had been cremated, in an attempt to "retain something from him."

Further proving how he had lost touch with reality, a few weeks later, his sister caught him watching her while she took a shower. Miyazaki attacked her when she demanded that he leave. When his mother found out and confronted him about the matter, he attacked her as well.

Miyazaki kept even more to himself and began collecting gory films, pornographic anime, child pornography, and adult magazines. He began to attend his college's tennis matches, not because he was interested in the sport, but so he could take photos up the women's skirts. He would use these photos to masturbate. He had a high libido, but that was coupled with being too self-conscious to speak to women his own age or older.

A high school classmate was asked to comment on what Miyazaki had been like in school and ended up divulging that Miyazaki had confided in him he had a small penis, which caused his insecurity and prevented him from approaching girls. The classmate went on to say he had always believed Miyazaki had an inferiority complex. Perhaps his inability to socialize with women his own age, combined with his high libido, was part of the reason why Miyazaki took advantage of little girls. He progressed quickly from avidly watching child pornography, which was legal in Japan at the time, to actively preying on children.

It was August 22, 1988. Miyazaki had celebrated his 26th birthday the prior day. That afternoon, four-year-old Mari Konno left her family's apartment in Saitama to play at a friend's house. A Nissan pulled up just as she left the apartment complex and a man got out of it. He convinced the girl to get in the car with him, then drove off. He ended up in a wooded area, under a bridge westward of Tokyo. He sat with Mari for half an hour before finally strangling her, then having sex with her corpse. He left her small, lifeless body in the hills near his home, but took her clothes home with him.

By that evening, when Mari had not returned home, her father, panic-stricken, called the police to report her missing. Despite all their efforts, Mari's body was not found. Miyazaki later returned to the crime scene, where Mari's corpse had been decomposing. He took her hands and feet, which he hid in his closet. He took the rest of her skeleton, save for her teeth, and placed it in his furnace. Once the bones had been successfully charred, he ground them into powder. He placed the ground bones in a box along with Mari's teeth and a photo of her clothes. He sent this box to her parents, alongside a note which read: "Mari. Cremated. Bones. Investigate. Prove."

October 3, 1988, Miyazaki was driving down a rural road in Hanno, Saitama, when he spotted seven-year-old Masami Yoshizawa walking alone. He offered her a ride, and she accepted. He drove her to the same place he had killed Mari. He strangled her, too, then had sex with her corpse. He left her in the same place he had left Mari, and once again took his victim's clothes home with him.

Miyazaki killed again on December 12, 1988. Four-year-old Erika Nanba was walking home from a friend's house when Miyazaki forcefully abducted her. He deviated from his typical routine and drove her to Naguri, Saitama, where he parked in a parking lot. He forced Erika to take off her clothes, then photographed her in the backseat of his car. He killed her, then tied her hands and feet behind her back. After placing a sheet over her body, he put her in the trunk of his car.

Once more straying from his usual tactics, he threw her clothes into a wooded area and disposed of her body in the nearby parking lot. One thing Miyazaki did not deviate from was taunting the girl's family. He sent them a letter compiled of different words from magazines, which spelled: "Erika. Cold. Cough. Throat. Rest. Death."

After the disappearance of Erika Nanba, the police immediately made the connection between her disappearance and that of Mari and Masami. Erika's clothes were found relatively quickly. The next day, her corpse was found. Suddenly, the investigation into the disappearance of the three girls took a dark turn. Law enforcement began to realize they potentially had a serial killer on their hands. All three girls lived in close proximity of each other, in Saitama Prefecture.

As they began to investigate the possibility that the person who murdered Erika may have also killed Mari and Masami, police learned all three families shared another experience. After each girl had gone missing, the family would receive strange phone calls. When answered, the caller on the other end would say nothing. If the family chose not to answer the eerie call, the phone would ring for at least twenty minutes.

It was on February 6, 1989, that Mari's father found the box with the ashes, photographs, and teeth. Originally, the verdict was that the teeth likely did not belong to Mari. When Miyazaki, who was following the news obsessively, heard this, he sent a letter to Mari's family entitled: "Crime Confession." He also included a photo of Mari. It was signed "Yuko Imada." A play on the words, "Now I'll tell." The letter stated: "I put the cardboard box with Mari's remains in it in front of her home. I did everything. From the start of the Mari incident to the finish. I saw the police press conference where they said the remains were not Mari's. On camera, her mother said the report gave her new hope that Mari might still be alive. I knew then that I had to write this confession, so Mari's mother would not continue to hope in vain. I say again: the remains are Mari's."

Finally, weeks later, definitive results came back that the teeth were indeed Mari's; two had been positively matched against the X-rays of her dental work. It was also confirmed that almost her entire skeleton lay, ground to dust, inside the box. Only her hands and feet were missing.

To make matters worse, her already distraught family received yet another letter from Miyazaki, who was still using the alias of "Yuko Imada." This one was titled: "Confession." It contained details of the changes Miyazaki had noted in Mari's body as it decomposed. Quite apparently, he had routinely gone back to visit her body. The letter stated things such as, "Before I knew it, the child's corpse had gone rigid. I wanted to cross her hands over her breast, but they would not budge." (sic)

He went on to describe the "red spots"—lividity??—that had appeared on Mari's body. "Big red spots. Like the Hinomaru flag. Or like you'd covered her whole body with red hanko seals. After a while, the body is covered with stretch marks. It was so rigid before, but now it feels like it's full of water. And it smells. How it smells. Like nothing you've ever smelled in this whole wide world."

On June 6, 1989, Miyazaki killed once more. He had managed to go nearly half a year since his last murder. This time, he approached five-year-old Ayako Nomoto and asked her if she would let him take pictures of her. After taking a few photographs, he led her to his car, where he killed her. He covered her body in a bedsheet before placing her in the trunk of his car. He took her body home. He spent two full days photographing, filming, and engaging in necrophilic acts with the corpse.

Once the body began to decompose, Miyazaki dismembered it. He dumped the torso in a cemetery and the head in the hills close by. He kept her hands, which he drank the blood from and ate part of. Two weeks later, he began to fear that police would find Ayako's torso and head, so he went back to retrieve them. Afterward, he kept them in his closet. Ayako Nomoto would be his last victim.

July 23, 1989. Tsutomu Miyazaki was in a park attempting to insert the zoom lens of a camera into a little girl's vagina. Luckily, before he succeeded, her father approached him. Despite being naked himself, Miyazaki decided to make a run for it. The girl's father promptly called the police. Miyazaki was arrested when he returned to retrieve his car.

The police believed they had caught the "Little Girl Murderer." When they searched Miyazaki's house, they found a collection of five thousand seven hundred and sixty-three videotapes. Scattered among the unbelievable amount of tapes were pictures and video footage of the victims. Also discovered were the body parts he had hidden away inside his home.

Once arrested, the long journey to a final trial and sentencing began. There are several differences between the criminal justice system in America versus that of Japan. Although Japan offers court-appointed attorneys for defendants who are unable to pay, court-appointed defense lawyers are notorious for rarely meeting with and interviewing their clients.

The quality of the defense strategy is measured by the amount of money a client can pay. It requires a lot of time to prepare a proper defense. Obtaining qualified professionals to look at the defendant's past mental health issues and background are important factors to an insanity defense—a fact often ignored by lawyers not being compensated for their time.

Miyazaki's father refused to pay for his son's defense. Ashamed and heartbroken that his offspring could commit such atrocious acts, he committed suicide in 1994. Upon hearing his father had taken his own life, Miyazaki stated he felt refreshed by the news and felt his father was justified for committing suicide; it was penance for doing such a terrible job parenting.

Unlike America, in Japan, even if the accused confesses to the crime, there must still be a full trial. Miyazaki's trial began in 1990, a time when Japan did not have jury trials. Instead, a judge, or a panel of judges, depending on the crime, listen to the evidence and make a ruling.

None of the mental health professionals who interviewed Miyazaki before his trial could draw any conclusions regarding his sanity with a high degree of certainty. Some thought his conversations and drawings of "Rat-Man," the persona Miyazaki blamed for forcing him to kill, were just a ruse. Other mental health professionals felt that Miyazaki was insane according to the legal definition, thereby not guilty of the crimes with which he was charged.

Seven years later, in 1997, Miyazaki's trial ended when a Tokyo District Court judge found him guilty of all charges and sentenced him to death. Japan's court system reviews cases of condemned persons at predetermined intervals to ensure a death sentence is still warranted.

Miyazaki appeared in court at two such trials in 2001 and again in 2006. The initial ruling was upheld, and Miyazaki was executed by hanging on June 17, 2008, at the age of forty-five.

V

Peter Niers

ALTHOUGH THE CHRISTIAN PROHIBITION ON magic dates back to Biblical times, for centuries, Christian authorities punished magic relatively mildly, with excommunication and exile, not execution, being the harshest penalties.

Punishment from secular authorities was generally limited to the magic that caused harm, otherwise known as "black magic." This changed in the thirteenth and fourteenth centuries, when all magic came to be deemed evil and a form of heresy. Acts against the church, or heresy, were automatically punishable by death.

The early fourteenth century witnessed the first trials, and executions, for black magic. While all were politically motivated, they helped establish, for the Church, the precedent of trying demonic magic as heresy. An educated, although biased, man, Pope John XXII, who had already charged many of his political opponents with the practice of black magic, convened a council of theologians in 1320.

His purpose was, once and for all, to determine the exact relationship between black magic and heresy. The council decided that black magic practitioners were indeed heretics, and the pope authorized inquisitors to act against them as such, giving them the power to inflict torture and even death on those found guilty.

Six years later, in 1326, the pope further strengthened the council's decision with the papal bull, Super illius specula. The bull condemned those who:

> *"sacrifice to demons, adore them, make images, rings, mirrors...for magic purposes, and...[bind] themselves in the most shameful slavery for the most shameful things. By their means a most pestilential disease, besides growing stronger and increasingly serious, grievously infects the flock of Christ throughout the world."*

The bull forbade all Christians from teaching, learning, or using demonic magic "by whatever means for whatever purpose." It gave Christians eight days to renounce such magic and turn in all magic texts for burning. Any who continued to practice would be subject to the same punishments as heretics, including automatic ex-communication or worse.

In the minds of medieval Europeans, demons stalked the world, sowing evil, and tempting humans to sin. Only with the help of God could these preternaturally powerful creatures be compelled to desist in their torment of humans.

A small group, consisting mostly of clerics, took this one step further, attempting to use that divine power to command demons for personal gain. To its practitioners, the very fact that black magic relied on the divine power of Christ made it an intrinsically pious and noble enterprise. Perhaps then, the practice of black magic was a logical outcome of orthodox medieval Christianity, an outcome no more irrational or immoral than anything else the church itself did.

However, medieval authorities never intended to let themselves be convinced of this. All institutions of power thrive only in the presence of an enemy, and until the medieval church helped invent the largely imagined practice of witchcraft, the very real practice of demoniac magic fit the bill quite nicely.

In fact, the "witch-craze" that swept through Europe, and later America, flowed directly from the condemnation of black magic. The foundation for the early modern witch trials was laid when religious authorities began to imagine Satanism and demonic pacts not just in the ritual magic with which they were familiar, but also in everyday "magic" and folk healings of common people.

Two hundred years after the papal bull of 1326, a bandit stood accused of allegiance with the devil. Branded a thief, murderer, cannibal, and heretic, the legend of Peter Niers still spreads its dark shadow across the pages of history.

Peter Niers was a German serial killer, cannibal, and bandit from the 16th century. In the fifteen years he was committing crimes, Niers reached legendary status, with rumors abound that he was in fact a practitioner of black magic who had received blessings from the Devil himself. All of medieval Europe was both fascinated with and appalled by his acts, and those frequenting the roads he and his gang of highwaymen haunted were in fear for their very lives.

Not only did he rob and kill travelers, but, under torture, he confessed to killing pregnant women and ripping their unborn children from their wombs, to eat, and also use parts in his magical spells. Many ballads about his horrific crimes and satanic practices were written after his initial arrest and subsequent escape. Niers, more legend than man, was executed in a brutal way.

His story highlights the brutality, mythological beliefs, and harshness of medieval Europe.

Niers was born into a time of unrest. His family were peasants in 16th century Germany, and he likely came of age during the German Peasants' War. Before the revolt, peasants who had once been freer than serfs were having serfdom forced upon them due to an increase in taxes, and the introduction of Roman civil law, which brought all the land in a territory into the power of the prince of the aristocratic dynasty ruling the area.

Serfs were among the lowest-ranking in feudal society. Most peasants held the status of a serf during this time period. Serfs were important to medieval society, but they were treated poorly, had little rights over their land, and often went hungry. However, they did have more rights than slaves. They were provided with protection and guaranteed justice by the lord of the manor they worked for and were able to live on his land so long as they worked it. Despite these few benefits, they were still treated poorly. They could not leave the land they were bound to, and if that land were to be sold, they would be sold along with it. Even if the lord of the manor did not have them work his land or provide him with produce, they would have to pay him in cash for his protection.

Roman civil law and heavy taxes were strongly beneficial to the princes of these dynasties because they were also being taxed, albeit by the Roman church, and many were breaking away from the church, beginning their own churches, to avoid being taxed. In order to make even more money, they would enforce the Roman civil law onto those peasants living in their territory, so their wealth would increase through the confiscation of the peasants' property and revenues.

The German Peasants' War began in 1524, near Alsace, where Peter Niers would later begin his criminal career. Alsace, France, is on the border of Germany, allowing Niers to commit crimes in both places. Niers was one of the leaders in a gang of highwaymen. Medieval roads typically ran from a town out into the forests and mountains, which were often dangerous. Due to the amount of coverage and good places to hide, bandits would often hijack carriages in these places, stealing anything of value and often murdering the travelers.

Peter Niers' group would lie in wait in places just outside of town, in forests such as these. The group eventually grew to contain twenty-four men, though they often worked in small groups, spreading themselves out all along the landscape in both France and Germany.

In 1577, a few of the gang members were caught in Gersbach, Germany, and, likely under torture, revealed the name of Peter Niers. Once Niers was arrested, he was subjected to the typical medieval torture. It is well-known that, in this time period, torture was commonly used to extract a confession from an unwilling prisoner. It was widely regarded as a legitimate means to obtain information about a crime the accused was thought to have committed, or to find out the names of accomplices. Under this torture, Niers confessed to seventy-five murders, some of which were deaths of local women. However, before anything else could happen to him, Niers managed to escape.

Now, Niers had certainly become a legend. First, he confessed to a large number of murders, but, in an even more wild twist, he escaped before justice could be served. It was then that rumors began to swirl about him. Supposedly, before his capture, Niers and his fellow bandits got together and called upon Satan himself. Satan met with them and, pleased with their acts, offered them his blessing, as well as financial support, paying them monthly.

Niers allegedly had the power to shapeshift at will. Niers was said to transform himself into either an animal or any inanimate object, often a rock or a log. However, there was one drawback to the shapeshifting abilities. Niers would have to keep a supply of human fetuses with him at all times. It was also said that Niers used the fat from infants to make candles that, when lit, would allow him to become invisible and enter peoples' homes at night without waking them.

Fetal parts were often associated with witches, and it was believed they were used to practice dark, potent magic. During the time of Niers' escape, the area had seen an increase in alleged witches. The only way for the medieval people to understand why a man would do such horrible things was to connect him, in this direct way, to Satan. Only a man who had denounced God and taken up with Satan would commit such heinous acts. The belief that Niers was, in fact, a black magician is reminiscent of Peter Stumpp, who would be executed only eight years later.

The story of Peter Stumpp is one in which the man who confessed may very well be innocent. In Bedburg, Germany, livestock were being ripped open, parts of them devoured, and left lying in the fields for those who owned them to find. However, it was not only livestock. The same began to happen to women and children in the area. The victims were strangled, bludgeoned, and disemboweled, in a way reminiscent if Jack the Ripper had been cruder and more careless. They had also been eaten raw. This was enough cause for concern for the citizens of Bedburg.

Peter Stumpp himself was a widower with two children, though rumors began to swirl that he was having an incestuous relationship with his sister and may have even impregnated his teenage daughter. The rumors were suspected to have started from a man whose wife had briefly been interested in Stumpp. However, that did not stop the gossip from spreading. The townspeople began to detest Stumpp. Matters got worse for Stumpp due to the fact that he had lost a hand years prior, and, shortly after the townspeople began to dislike him, a wolf's paw was found in a trap. The community began to wonder if Stumpp was in fact a werewolf. Furthermore, Stumpp was a Protestant, in a time when Catholicism was trying to choke out Protestantism.

The people in Stumpp's town fully believed it was a werewolf who had murdered these people and butchered the livestock. While out hunting for the werewolf, the hounds being used caught the scent of something and began to chase it down, only for it to be none other than Peter Stumpp. Stumpp was quickly captured. Under torture, he began to confess to not only murder, but also to being a werewolf.

He claimed the Devil had given him a magical belt when he was twelve, allowing him to shapeshift into a wolf. The day he was captured, he had tossed the belt into the bushes. He confessed to killing and cannibalizing fourteen children and multiple women. He said he had eaten the hearts of unborn children after ripping them from their mothers' wombs. He also admitted to not only impregnating his daughter, but to killing his own son and having a sexual relationship with a succubus sent to him by the Devil.

He was executed brutally, as were his daughter and the woman he had been supposedly sleeping with.

While Peter Niers may have been completely guilty of the murders, it is also possible that he was scapegoated. Nevertheless, he played upon the fears of those in his town of werewolves and satanic things. The superstitions of the area were also repeated in

Niers' story. Those around him could not understand why he committed such evil acts. Like with Peter Stumpp, the only possible explanation for his being willing to commit such atrocities was that he was, in fact, in league with the Devil and additionally had some magical powers. Stumpp could only possibly be a shapeshifter in these peoples' eyes, and it was the same with Niers years earlier.

Yet another ballad detailed how he was recognized and subsequently captured. Niers was lodging in an inn called "The Bells" in Neumarkt. He went to a bathhouse a couple of days later after deciding he wanted to wash himself. By this point, his description had been circulated through pamphlets and warrants. When Niers left the inn, he handed his personal bag over to the innkeeper, saying it was valuable, and he did not want to lose it. At the bathhouse, while he was soaking, people around him began to whisper. He did not notice it at all. Those in the room recognized him as Peter Niers, and two people went to the inn where he had been staying. When they informed the innkeeper who exactly he was letting stay in his inn, the innkeeper began to wonder about the satchel Niers had given to him.

Apparently, the innkeeper opened the satchel and discovered it full of hands and hearts of fetuses. The townspeople, enraged by the contents of the satchel, began to formulate a plan to capture

Niers. They sent eight strong men to the bathhouse to capture him. He came along without causing trouble, defeated at last. It was rumored the only reason he was recognized and captured so easily was that he had been separated from the fetus parts in his satchel. He eventually confessed to having murdered five hundred forty-four people.

The execution of Peter Niers was an incredibly brutal one. It was detailed in a popular ballad from the time. People from all around the region gathered to watch. On the first day, strips of his flesh were peeled from his body, and then hot oil was poured into the wounds. On the second day, the bottoms of his feet were coated in grease, then held above hot coals, thereby roasting him alive. On the third day, he was placed on the breaking wheel.

The breaking wheel was a large, spoked wheel similar to that used on carts and carriages, and a common form of execution in this time period, though its use continued as late as the 19th century in Germany. In Niers' time, it was often used as punishment for those convicted of murder though the exact method of execution varied from region to region.

The point of execution by the breaking wheel was mutilation and a slow, agonizing death, which was considered a just punishment for those convicted of heinous murders. Because the torture was to be prolonged, it frequently began with the wheel being dropped onto the shins first. The executioner would then work his way up the legs, then crush the forearms, then the upper arms. The exact number of blows to be delivered was prescribed specifically for each individual case. Occasionally, though not often, the executioner could be ordered to execute the criminal in this first act once the limbs had been broken by aiming for the neck or heart. Even more rarely, the executioner was ordered to begin directly with the neck or heart. The breaking wheel was even used in North America as a form of execution for slaves involved in revolts during the 18th century.

When the forty bone-shattering blows did not kill Niers, he was then quartered. He died that day, September 16, 1581.

Just a few years later, Peter Stumpp would also be brutally executed for the serial murders he was convicted of. Stumpp's execution purposely took place on Halloween in 1589. Once strapped to the breaking wheel, Stumpp also had his flesh peeled from his body, then his limbs broken. He was then beheaded, and his head was placed on a pole carved to look like a wolf. His daughter and mistress were flayed alive, then strangled, after which their bodies were thrown onto the pyre alongside Stumpp's and burned.

Confessions of serial killers from the medieval period are some of the most shocking of all, with staggeringly high body counts and acts of diabolical sadism. It is important, however, to remember that these confessions were made under torture. Niers was certainly a murderer and a thief, but it is impossible to say exactly how many victims he claimed, or if any of the tales of fetus-eating were true.

Additionally confusing is the fabrications weaved into folklore and ballads about his alleged magical abilities, for, with all those tall tales and confessing under torture, how is one to know what exactly Peter Niers did or did not do?

None are alive today, over four hundred years later, will ever know for sure how many lives Niers claimed, but it is certain that his larger-than-life story of crime, cannibalism, black magic, and murder will live on through the ages.

VI

Alexander Spesivtsev

PERHAPS AMERICANS HAVE A SOMEWHAT distorted image of Russia, one warped by stereotypes based on characters created by literary legends such as Dostoevsky. "Russia" often brings to mind images of desolate Siberia, endless breadlines, and brooding men in moral and ethical conflict as they struggle to feed their family.

It is almost as if, intuitively, we hear of a Russian murderer and think, "Ah, yes, that hard, bitter existence life has forced them to eke out has finally caused them to snap." It is not a pardon for their sins, merely something deep at the core of a person that allows one to relate to an individual doing anything to provide for their family.

Serial killers, in general, developed a much more sympathetic face after the popular TV show, Dexter, introduced the world to a relatively unknown brand of killer—the vigilante serial killer. Somehow, if the murderer in question is handsome, and the viewers believe his deeds are noble, serial murder is much more widely accepted. Most people would likely welcome the opportunity to rid the world of drug dealers, who trade their wares for the food stamps a drug-dependent single mother should be using to feed her baby, and the predators and pimps who peddle child sex and child pornography.

These circumstances seem almost justified, but not according to the law. Two wrongs, do in fact, not make a right. When Russian serial killer Alexander Spesivtsev was apprehended in 1996, he made a bold pronouncement; his crimes were a statement and protest against the newly democratic state, and what it stood for.

Politics has always been a powder keg, often leading to war, and war, by its very nature, begets killing. But using political protest as an excuse to murder seems less plausible, especially if the perpetrator has a dying teen on the couch, her beheaded friend in the bathroom, and the discarded ribcage of yet another victim in the living room.

At that point, it would be difficult to make anyone believe the killings were a noble action in response to an evil faction. Spesivtsev and his mother readily admitted to cannibalism, using the excuse the victims were disenfranchised youth and doomed to a far worse fate than becoming someone's dinner.

During a chaotic time, a man with chaotic, violent desires decided to use his philosophy as a weapon with which to cut down society's most vulnerable. Alexander Spesivtsev believed homeless children were the manifestation of the problems with democracy. He and his mother, Lyudmila, offered the children a place to stay out of the frigid Siberian weather. They were his prey and he was the predator, drawing them into his trap like a spider in its web. Once inside the family's hellish apartment, the children would never escape the clutches of the "Cannibal of Siberia."

Novokuznetsk, Russia, was once a small, sleepy town located in Kemerovo Oblast, in southwestern Siberia. The peacefulness of the town was quickly replaced by Joseph Stalin's industrialization of the Soviet Union. Novokuznetsk became a bustling major coal mining and industrial center. Unfortunately, after the fall of communism, production began to slow and less and less material was being manufactured.

The town faltered and began to fail under democracy. By the time in which the crimes of Alexander Spesivtsev took place, the five immense steelworks in Novokuznetsk were no longer causing the sky to become dark with smoke. The surrounding coal mining towns had gone bankrupt. The people in the area were not being paid regularly.

The streets were full of homeless children—runaways, drifters, dropouts—all begging to get by, living in cellars, or wherever they could find shelter. Generally, they went unnoticed by the adults in Novokuznetsk, who were too consumed with their own problems of poverty. The only adults who typically took note of these street children were police, and that was only to break up the groups and hustle them along. That is, until Alexander Spesivtsev came along.

When looking at these children, he saw what he believed to be an example of how democracy had failed. To him, they were the embodiment of all its evils. In his eyes, these children would grow up to be prostitutes and drug addicts. They were forever doomed to be a blemish on society. He would protest against democracy by taking their lives.

Alexander Nikolayevich Spesivtsev, sometimes known as Sasha, was born March 1, 1970, into a dysfunctional household.

His father was abusive and would take turns beating each member of the family. Alexander was a weak and sickly child. His mother, Lyudmila Spesivtsev, was very protective and doting toward him. The two even shared a bed until Alexander was twelve.

Alexander was an asocial child who did not make many friends and was often bullied. His mother frequently showed him pictures from true crime books, which seemed to have imprinted on his psyche. As he got older, he began to grow violent and sadistic. As a young adult, he seemed headed to repeat his father's abusive actions, with his girlfriend as the target. He eventually killed her in 1991 and was then sent to a mental institution.

Once released, Spesivtsev moved into an apartment with his mother and his dog. The apartment was rundown and covered in graffiti, with elevators and lights that only sometimes worked. It was there that he lured his victims in order to execute his sadistic desires. His mother also aided him by luring victims in, offering them food or payment in exchange for work.

Lyudmila was easy for the children to trust. She certainly seemed motherly enough. Additionally, through her work at the local school, she had become good with children. Even if it was Alexander who went on the prowl, the children would still follow him home. They were hungry and desperate to get out of the freezing night air.

Once the children followed either one home, however, they were trapped. If they tried to escape, they would have to make it through Alexander, his mother, and their large, fierce dog.

Alexander would proceed to rape, torture, and kill the victims. His mother would cook their flesh, and the two would sit down and have it for dinner. The next day, Lyudmila would take body parts with her and toss them into the Aba River as she passed it.

As time went on, the family's neighbors began to notice that something was definitely amiss. A horrible stench, coupled with blaring rock music, emanated from the apartment. The neighbors reported it to the police multiple times, but nothing ever came of it. Law enforcement viewed it simply as a cleanliness problem, certainly nothing indicative of homicide.

Had they looked up the man living in that apartment and discovered he had committed homicide in the past, they may have put more weight into the complaints, but they did not even do that much. The police did take notice of the body parts that were coming to the surface of the Aba River. It was then they came to the realization there was a serial killer in the area.

Who that killer was would not be discovered until a plumber came to visit the Spesivtsev apartment four months later.

A plumber had been called on to figure out what was wrong with the pipes in the dingy apartment complex. He eventually traced the problem back to Lyudmila Spesivtsev's apartment. Relieved to almost be through with his task, he knocked at the apartment door. To his dismay, nobody answered. He continued to knock until his knocks grew into bangs and, angered, he called the police. As the police entered the apartment, Spesivtsev climbed out the window. The police did not follow suit. They were too shocked by what they saw in the living room.

They were confronted by the sight of a teenage girl lying on the couch, her abdomen covered in stab wounds and blood soaking her as well as the couch. In the middle of the floor lay a human ribcage. In the bathroom, was a headless torso in the bathtub. In the kitchen, there were human remains in bowls. Blood covered the walls, along with piles of bloodstained clothes everywhere.

The girl was fifteen-year-old Olga Galtseva, who had disappeared with two thirteen-year-old friends. Police had ignored the girls' parents' pleas to find them. Dismissing the parents' concerns, they insisted the girls had likely run away with boys, to party, drink, and do drugs.

However, that was not the case. Olga told police that she and her friends had gone out to buy batteries when they encountered Lyudmila Spesivtsev. The woman was carrying several shopping bags. Seeing how she was struggling to carry them, the girls decided to help Lyudmila take them home. Once there, they were cornered by Alexander Spesivtsev and his ferocious dog.

One girl was stabbed to death and the other two were forced to dismember her in the bathtub and then dine on her flesh. Then, the dog had attacked the second girl, killing her. Olga was eventually stabbed as well. She lived for only seventeen hours before dying from her injuries.

Alexander Spesivtsev was found in a woman's apartment, where he had fled and was attempting to rape, and was apprehended before he was able to complete the crime.

When police searched the mother's apartment, they found decomposing body parts amidst the piles of clothes. They discovered eighty-two articles of clothing, forty pieces of jewelry, and photographs of unknown people. They did not attempt to identify any of the body parts. The parents of the girls who went missing with Olga felt that their daughters' remains went undiscovered and unidentified due to their being in the lower class of society.

Police did not dig for bodies at first and explained it away by saying they would wait until the snow had melted. They also explained away the lack of genetic testing done on the articles of clothing by having a lack of funds, which is highly probable.

The killings and cannibalism did not draw the attention of most people, as it surely would have in a different place. In fact, most people outside of Novokuznetsk did not even know who Alexander Spesivtsev was. Brutal killings, unfortunately, were fairly common in the country, almost always among the poor, the unemployed, the uneducated, or anyone else of the bottom rung of society. Cannibalism was certainly not unheard of; it was especially common in Siberia to hear on the news that someone had been arrested for killing and eating someone else, though before it had usually been one-time incidents.

Additionally, most people in Novokuznetsk who had not been directly affected by the murders tended to ignore it. They had bigger problems. The social castes in Russia were so deeply divided that no newspaper in the big city had even reported of Alexander

Spesivtsev's crimes. The social classes were so deeply divided between the haves and the have-nots that street children preyed upon did not even concern the upper class.

The investigation was slow and drawn-out, with law enforcement dawdling and generally placing it on the back burner. The families of known victims worried about the sway Spesivtsev's sister, Nadezhda, might have held over the investigation. She worked as the secretary for a local judge, and Lyudmila had actually worked there at one point, as well. In fact, neighbors saw Nadezhda going into the apartment during the time which the three girls were being held there. She was given psychiatric tests and freed in no time at all.

It was discovered during the investigation that Spesivtsev had dealings in the black market. Not only did he have a source of income—albeit an illegal one—but so did his mother. He had also written books about philosophy while in mental institutions, as well as his critical views on democracy. His being an author led to investigators referring to him as an "intellectual." Additionally discovered in a search of the apartment was a diary belonging to Spesivtsev. Its entries detailed nineteen murders. This would be the prosecution's key piece of evidence.

Though it was speculated that Spesivtsev had killed at least eighty people, judging by the number of clothes in his home, it could only be proven that he had killed the nineteen detailed in his diary. Spesivtsev was ruled insane and committed to a mental institution once more.

His mother, Lyudmila, was sentenced to thirteen years in prison for acting as an accomplice.

During her time in prison and even after her release, Lyudmila never spoke about the murders. She has since virtually dropped off the face of the earth. Spesivtsev, however, still remains in the institution. He bides his time writing poetry as well as more books about philosophy and the evils of democracy.

When asked how he could even attempt to justify his crimes, he shrugged and said, "How many people has our democracy destroyed? If people thought about that, there would not be any of this filth. But what can you do?"

He once asked if a reporter might be able to arrange for the sale of his head, more aptly his brain, so that scientists could study it after he died. He asked to be paid in advance, of course, and for the payment to be in cigarettes.

According to experts, Americans with violent urges or deviant desires might commit such things as rape, child abuse, and sexual harassment. Russians interact socially, as classes or groups, and so a Russian with violent urges may commit acts of an antisocial nature, such as cannibalism.

It is also highly possible that, just like any of the other cannibals in this book, Alexander Spesivtsev simply had the desire to consume his victims.

The thought process of Alexander Spesivtsev is not easy to understand. From his reasoning for killing to his motives for cannibalism, it is one long train wreck of mental instability and psychopathic desires.

We may never know how many children met their grisly demise in that rundown, horrific apartment.

Conclusion

IN CONCLUSION, CANNIBALISM REMAINS A TABOO matter for most people in modern times. Although it has its place in history, most of us prefer it to stay there—in the past.

As a means of survival, it is perhaps understandable, but thankfully, few people will ever be faced with that decision.

Consensual cannibalism, whether it is legalized or not, is not something the general population is interested in pursuing, although it has been claimed that an estimated 800 cannibals currently reside in Germany alone.

Laws are created to protect the majority, and in an age where groceries can be ordered via the worldwide web, I, for one, prefer to order food from an online grocer rather than shop for human flesh in a Cannibal Café.

Acknowledgments

This is a special thanks to the following readers who have taken time out of their busy schedule to be part of True Crime Seven Team. Thank you all so much for all the feedbacks and support!

Steve Johnson, Bonnie Kernene, Sandra M. Van Domelen, Pat Eroh, Catherine Douglass, Morene Rehbine, Muhammad Nizam Mohtar, Naomi Burney, Dani Binger, Luann Larscheid, Phyllis Carlin, Susan Margaret Leedy

Continue Your Exploration Into

The Murderous Minds

Excerpt From Murderous Minds Volume 4

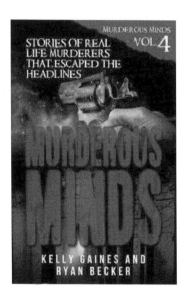

I
Michael Cleary

'*ARE YOU A WITCH
Or are you a fairy*

Or are you the wife of Michael Cleary'

An old Irish children's rhyme can still be heard on playgrounds across Europe, but the story behind the silly song is no matter of lighthearted fun.

In March of 1895, a religious, law-abiding Irish man murdered his wife in front of their family and friends. The man, Michael

Cleary, did not believe he was committing murder. He did not believe he was in any way harming his beloved wife, Bridget.

To Michael, his actions were the last effort in saving his wife from a terrible fate. He believed, against the advice of doctors and priests, that the creature he was killing was not his Bridget. He believed it was a fairy—a changeling masquerading as Bridget—while the real Mrs. Cleary remained trapped in another realm.

In the days leading up to the brutal attack, the Cleary home had dissolved into chaos. Bonds of trust between family, friends, church officials, and medical professionals were pushed to their limit. Michael Cleary became a startling example of what can happen when religious vigor, old-world superstition, and evolving ideas about the roles of women collide.

To understand Michael Cleary's crime, you have to understand what fueled his impossible beliefs. The world was changing for Ireland in 1895, and that terrifying frontier of progress broke apart a young couple's marriage and a community's trust.

Bridget Boland married cooper Michael Cleary in August of 1887. She was a bright, lovely, talented young woman with charm enough to win her any husband she wanted. The man she wanted, Michael, was a working-class man and devout Catholic.

As a cooper, he made barrels, wooden casks, and other goods created from local timber. Michael had been trained as an apprentice to make his wares by hand, a skill that was quickly becoming overshadowed by the industrial boom and more efficient means of creating and distributing products.

Even so, it seems Michael did not have a difficult time making a match with the vibrant Bridget Boland. Their marriage was one of mutual love—Bridget seeing a worthy and loving partner in Michael and Michael seeing a sweet and virtuous girl in Bridget.

From all accounts, the early days of their marriage were normal. Michael was a hard worker with a determination to provide for his beautiful new bride and make a name for himself.

While Bridget had a good deal of care and respect for her husband, she was not satisfied with the traditional "woman's work" in the home. Bridget took up work as a dressmaker's apprentice, a decision that kindled a small bit of friction between the couple.

Working women may have been more common at this time than they had been in decades past, but it was a concept still shunned by more conservative households. This was especially true for the traditional Catholic families of Ireland. Michael was not making enough to support him and Bridget in the way he wanted, but he was still adamant that a wife should stay home—not worry herself with a career outside of the home. This notion was problematic. Bridget's skill as a dressmaker offered a possibility for the family to live comfortably, if not very well off. She had no intention of letting her abilities go to waste in the interest of satisfying her husband's old-fashioned sensitivity.

Not long after their marriage, Bridget returned to her parent's house in Ballyvadlea. Michael stayed behind in Clonmel, to finish up his current affairs as a cooper. Michael wanted desperately to prove to Bridget he was capable of fulfilling the long-accepted role as a husband and sole breadwinner. Unbeknownst to him, Bridget had expanded her career since leaving Clonmel. She continued her dressmaking after purchasing a Singer sewing machine.

At the time, the Singer model was state of the art. It offered women a chance to produce quickly and venture into the world of business. The same technological boom that was making men like Michael obsolete, was giving their wives more opportunities outside of the home. Michael wasn't the only man in Ireland bothered by the uptick in women's professions, but the prospect of not having to scrape by in poverty seemed to win out in many households. Unfortunately for Michael, dressmaking was not the only job Bridget had taken on.

She bought and kept her own flock of chickens, and made decent money selling the eggs to friends and neighbors. This meant taking long walks in rain or shine across the moors to customers.

If there is a defining detail to mark where the tables began to turn between Michael and Bridget, her daily trek across the moors sparked the fire that would turn into a full-on blaze of superstition. The Irish moors, much like the English moors, were thought to be more than just vast empty wetlands. These flat expanses of fog and marsh were the subject of centuries of Irish folklore. Thought to hide entryways into the realm of the fairies, these desolate spaces were filled with tales of dangerous creatures and mischievous tricksters.

Irish children were raised to be wary of them. Those that held tight to the old Irish superstitions and folk beliefs thought it possible for someone to disappear into the fog and be spirited away by unnatural creatures. Michael Cleary was one of these believers.

Fairies of old Irish mythology were not kind, flower-wearing creatures who sprinkled magic dust and granted wishes. Irish fairies were tricksters, kidnappers, instigators, and monsters. In some legends, fairies destroyed homes and crops when they felt insulted.

In others, they would spirit away young virgins to corrupt their purity.

The most famous fairy lore was much more frightening. The story of the changelings was a very real concern in old-world Ireland. Legend claimed that if a loved one, adult or child, began to behave out of character, it was likely they were not their loved one at all. These changes indicated the presence of a changeling—a fairy sent to take the place of a human while the real human was kidnapped to the fairy realm.

Changeling trials were, for a time, a popular branch of witch hysteria in old Europe. It was believed these creatures were evil, and casting them out of the community was the only way to restore virtue and balance. Unfortunately, the methods for removing a changeling were often violent and dangerous. Suspected changelings could be beaten, burned, held over fire, or underwater, and in some cases poisoned by concoctions of deadly plants such as foxglove.

By the 1890s, much of Ireland had turned from belief in these horrific methods. The Catholic Church even began to dissuade followers from giving in to the hysteria of such superstitions and the dangers they could bring. Still, some refused to let go of the fairy realm.

There were still men and women believed to be "fairy doctors"—individuals skilled in providing medical treatment when a supernatural creature or ailment was the cause. Bridget's own cousin, Jack Dunne, was one of these so-called doctors. Those who believed in the dangers of the fairy realm relied on men like Dunn for help, but also kept an arsenal of old folk protections on hand to circumvent the possibility of a supernatural attack.

There were safety precautions one could take to avoid the misfortune of fairies. Many learned to leave them bowls of milk and sugar to keep them satisfied. Others would leave out small gifts and offerings in hopes of appeasing the fairies and avoiding their ire. You could also adorn your home with iron objects, as the belief that fairies were repelled by iron was commonly accepted.

Above all these things, the most important way to avoid a tangle with the fairies was to stay out of the moors, and far away from the fairy rings. Fairy rings were circles made of natural items and thought to function as a doorway to the fairy realm. A naturally occurring circle of mushrooms, trees, or even rocks was thought to be a dangerous place. Many avoided them altogether, but some brave souls went to the fairy rings on purpose in hopes of summoning the creatures to ask for a favor, or more morbidly, speak to the dead.

Some of the supposed fairy rings had much more explainable and logical origins. Many were later proven to be the remnants of long-forgotten man-made structures that had eroded over time to resemble circular imprints of stone and other leftover material. Ballyvadlea had many of these old circles, which slowly, little by little, townsfolk had begun to disregard.

When Michael eventually left Clonmel to join his wife in Ballyvadlea, he was horrified to learn of Bridget's professional advancement. The realization that her new business also took her on frequent trips through the dreaded moors shook Michael to his core and planted a seed of paranoia that had not existed in their marriage before.

To make matters worse, after the death of Bridget's mother, the couple assumed care of her elderly father, Patrick Boland. Once a laborer, Patrick was able to provide the family with fine accommodations in a labor village. It was said he acquired the nicest house in the village for his small family. But it wasn't cunning or luck that afforded Boland the lovely new home. The other families in the village had no interest in the house, many rejecting the opportunity to live there. The aversion came from a widely accepted local legend—the Boland house was built on the site of a fairy ring.

The labor village was full of older and less educated families, making it a community still primed for fear in the old legends. This information haunted Michael. His wife's differing views were difficult to accept, but their proximity to dangerous fairy rings gave him the perfect excuse for Bridget's behavior. It is likely that Michael began to suspect their fairy folk were to blame for his troubles from the moment he arrived in Ballyvadlea.

His firm belief in the superstitious legends of old and devout Catholicism made him feel as though he were a champion of righteousness in a world clouded by dark forces. These beliefs grew stronger as Bridget flourished, mixing with his mounting frustration of not finding steady work while his wife became more successful, a deadly storm was brewing inside Michael Cleary.

In March of 1895, Bridget went out to make her normal rounds delivering to customers. She intended to check in on her cousin, Jack Dunne, who lived across the moors when her work was done and return home afterward. Michael was in a foul mood that day. Still struggling to find work, as well as jealous and confused by his wife's success, it is believed that Michael and Bridget fought that morning over baseless accusations of adultery.

Michael had a lot of time on his hands, and most of it was spent tormenting himself over what his wife was up to when she was out of the house. He worried about the fairies and became enraged and embarrassed that Bridget was effectively the family's provider.

Even if Bridget suggested Michael join her on the delivery route, he refused. To Michael Cleary, the only thing worse than staying home while your wife worked was working with her in a business she created. Michael believed Bridget was changing. He may not have been completely wrong.

Reports from some who knew the couple claimed he criticized her hours away from home, methods of prayer, and choice in clothing—even taking issue with the undergarments she chose to wear. Michael's idea of a proper wife was set in stone, and there was no room for a woman looking to change and progress.

Difficult as their home life was becoming, there is no evidence to suggest that Bridget was interested in anything other than finding balance with her troubled husband. She was an evolving independent woman, yes, but she still held tight to her Catholic faith and believed in the sanctity of her marriage. Bridget decided not to back down and bend to Michael's will. As far as she was concerned, he was more than welcome at her side. If he would prefer to sulk at home all day, that was his choice.

In the days leading up to her murder, Bridget had fallen ill. She was suffering from a sore throat and terrible coughing fits that were made worse by long treks through cold wetlands. Still, illness would not keep Bridget from her work. The day she set out to visit Jack Dunne, Bridget's symptoms seem to have escalated. She became disoriented while wandering through the moors and was said to have been lost for several hours before stumbling home.

Her father and Michael were present when she finally arrived. Her father was concerned and urged her to get to bed, but Michael was completely horrified at her condition. The sick woman was confused, fevered, and clearly in need of medical attention. The stuttering, sickly woman struggling to stand up on her own did not resemble the Bridget Cleary Michael knew.

To most, these would be clear signs of a severe illness. To the frustrated and suppressed Mr. Cleary, the symptoms were signifiers of something else. If Michael had been harboring any deep desire to harm Bridget, this had given him the perfect excuse.

Michael and Patrick sent for a doctor, though Michael believed he already knew what was wrong with his wife. The woman had returned from known fairyland, acting strangely and almost inhuman. This couldn't be Bridget. Without input from Patrick, Michael sent for another person to diagnose Bridget's condition—her fairy doctor cousin, Jack Dunne. There are conflicting reports as to whether or not Michael initially sent for a medical doctor in the first place, or simply told his father-in-law he had.

At this period in Ireland, most villages had few, if any, doctors. If someone fell ill, a doctor had to be sent for. The journey could take precious days, which it did in Bridget's case. Some neighbors believed Michael had sent for Jack instead, only relenting to call for a real doctor at the anger and insistence of Patrick.

In either case, Jack Dunne arrived and examined Bridget. His diagnosis confirmed Michael's superstitious fears. The woman in his home was not even a real woman; it was an evil fairy changeling.

Jack and Michael got to work planning folk cures to dispel the changeling. If Patrick was skeptical at first, the urging of both his nephew and son-in-law eventually swayed him. Within a day, he had decided to help the other men with their nonsensical mission.

Patrick would claim he truly had begun to believe Bridget was in danger.

The medical doctor arrived days later and diagnosed Bridget with a severe case of Bronchitis. He noted the woman to be in terrible condition and took note of the tense atmosphere within the Cleary home. He prescribed medication for Bridget and gave her husband strict instructions on how to administer it. She was ill enough that a priest, Father Ryan, was called to the home to deliver communion and last rites.

The decision may have seemed like a normal precaution in a devout Catholic community, but it would later serve as key evidence to how badly Bridget was treated and how seemingly intentionally her sickness had been allowed to progress.

During the later trial, Father Ryan testified that when he arrived at the Cleary home, Bridget was conscious, alive, and agitated. Michael explained to him that though the doctor had prescribed her medicine to treat the Bronchitis, he would not give it to her. He told the priest, "People may have some remedy of their own that might do more good than doctor's medicine."

Father Ryan was unsettled by Cleary's words and encouraged him to follow the doctor's orders and not be overcome by fairy mythology. Ryan believed that medical care, not magic, was in Bridget's best interest. Michael did not agree. Father Ryan left the home that evening, having been unable to convince Michael.

According to changeling mythology, once a loved one has been taken, there are only nine days to save them. If left un-rescued past the ninth day, they are the fairies forever. This meant that Michael was on a deadline if he ever wanted to see his wife again. Doctor's orders and the priest's urging meant little to him. Michael believed that these other treatments were wasting time, allowing the unholy creature to exist longer in his wife's place.

As days ticked by, Bridget was defiant as ever. Being close to death did not stop the willful young woman from standing her ground. No matter the torture, she refused to admit any wrongdoing.

Michael's methods of "treatment" became more severe, an observation which began to disturb some of the friends and family who visited the house in those days. Patrick was among the disturbed, eventually believing the changeling must be gone and Bridget already returned.

Sadly, there was little the loving but frail father could do to help his daughter. The old man was no match for Michael, whose anger, frustration, and tension had come to a boiling point. To make matters worse, Jack actively fueled Michael's mounting paranoia, offering another extreme "cure" each time one seemed to fail.

During these supernatural treatments, the sick woman was held down and forced to drink a tonic of urine. When that did not yield results that satisfied Michael, he tormented her with items heated by the fire. As Bridget struggled, Michael shouted at her to submit and confess to being a changeling. Bridget held her ground, even as the consequences became more deadly.

Bridget's attending loved ones assisted Michael in many of the initial attacks. Both her father and cousin were reported to have helped hold her down when the urine tonic was used—despite the horrified woman was screaming and pleading through a Bronchitis-riddled throat.

By the time Bridget was a few days into her illness, her family had begun to doubt there was a supernatural cause at all. It became difficult to justify the cruelty, especially when the victim was a person—at least physically—they had known and cared for. It is unclear exactly why her family did not put a stop to Michael's behavior.

On the final day of Bridget's life, Michael is reported to have demanded that she admit to being a fairy impostor one last time, a deadly amount of anger rising within him. Bridget, though badly beaten and still sick, refused. No matter how much Michael screamed and threatened, Bridget was determined to stand her ground.

In a fit of rage, Michael lifted Bridget by her neck and threw her onto the stones in front of the fireplace. He then poured lamp oil over her and set her nightgown on fire. Bridget's father and other family members witnessed the event. The poor woman, who was still recovering from her real sickness, was burned in front of an audience whom she had once believed loved her.

Whether or not Bridget was burned alive is still a point of debate. The court was unable to determine if Bridget died when her head hit the stone floor or if she was killed by the fire, but the result was clear—Bridget Cleary had been murdered in cold blood at the hands of her husband.

Witnesses gave varied reports as to what happened next in the Cleary home. Authorities could confirm that Michael and Jack took Bridget's burned corpse out of the house and buried her in a shallow grave nearby. They reported the death to no one. Bridget's family recalled Michael keeping vigil on the property. He was seemingly waiting for his wife to arrive back home, saved by his valiant defeat of the fairies.

On March 22, 1895, her body was discovered in a shallow grave after neighbors reported she had been missing for several days. Ten people were arrested for the crime, including Michael. Of the ten, all but Michael were freed of the charge of murder, but four were convicted of "wounding."

The trial gained international attention, prompting the media to dub Bridget, "the last witch burned in Ireland." Some news outlets used the case as justification for terrible Irish stereotypes.

As if the tragic end to her life was not enough, Bridget became a cautionary tale meant to insult her own people. The media claimed that her murder was proof of the Irish being an uneducated and backward people incapable of governing themselves without descending into superstitious chaos. The coverage added insult to injury, and more often than not, failed to give any respect to the young woman that had been senselessly cut down in the prime of her life.

Michael showed no remorse for the killing. Those present at his trial were horrified to hear witnesses claim that even as her body burned, he continued to shout it was only a changeling, and the creature's death would bring his wife back to him. The arresting officers would testify that Michael was incredulous during his arrest. He seemed completely certain Bridget would step back through the fairy ring any day now and the entire mess would be cleared up.

Fairies, magic, the evil beyond the veil, were all real to Michael Cleary. He was convinced he had done his community a favor by dispelling a dangerous force. With or without fairy lore, that is likely exactly what Michael believed.

Michael Cleary spent fifteen years in prison on the charge of manslaughter. There is no evidence he ever apologized for, or admitted, killing his wife.

After his release, Michael is recorded to have immigrated to Canada where he disappeared from public record. What happened in the Cleary home during that terrible spring of 1895 will never be completely revealed.

Why did Bridget's family go along with Michael?

Why did they stand by for so long?

How did one man murder his wife in front of a group of people who supposedly cared for her, without significant challenge?

The answers are long gone, laid to rest with Bridget, but perhaps the answer lies in belief. Horrific things are possible if you can sway others to believe in impossible things.

The End of **The Preview**

Visit us at **truecrimeseven.com** or scan QR Code using your phone's **camera app** to find more true crime books and other cool goodies.

  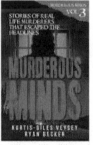 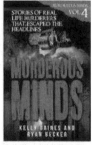

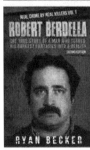 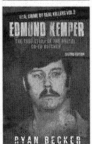  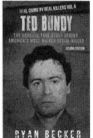

About True Crime Seven

True Crime Seven is about exploring the stories of the sinful minds in this world. From unknown murderers to well-known serial killers. It is our goal to create a place for true crime enthusiasts to satisfy their morbid curiosities while sparking new ones.

Our writers come from all walks of life but with one thing in common, and that is they are all true crime enthusiasts. You can learn more about them below:

Ryan Becker is a True Crime author who started his writing journey in late 2016. Like most of you, he loves to explore the process of how individuals turn their darkest fantasies into a reality. Ryan has always had a passion for storytelling. So, writing is the best output for him to combine his fascination with psychology and true crime. It is Ryan's goal for his readers to experience the full immersion with the dark reality of the world, just like how he used to in his younger days.

Nancy Alyssa Veysey is a writer and author of true crime books, including the bestselling, Mary Flora Bell: The Horrific True Story Behind an Innocent Girl Serial Killer. Her medical degree and work in the field of forensic psychology, along with postgraduate studies in criminal justice, criminology, and pre-law, allow her to bring a unique perspective to her writing.

Kurtis-Giles Veysey is a young writer who began his writing career in the fantasy genre. In late 2018, he parlayed his love and knowledge of history into writing nonfiction accounts of true crime stories that occurred in centuries past. Told from a historical perspective, Kurtis-Giles brings these victims and their killers back to life with vivid descriptions of these heinous crimes.

Kelly Gaines is a writer from Philadelphia. Her passion for storytelling began in childhood and carried into her college career. She received a B.A. in English from Saint Joseph's University in 2016, with a concentration in Writing Studies. Now part of the real world, Kelly enjoys comic books, history documentaries, and a good scary story. In her true-crime work, Kelly focuses on the motivations of the killers and backgrounds of the victims to draw a complete picture of each individual. She deeply enjoys writing for True Crime Seven and looks forward to bringing more spine-tingling tales to readers.

James Parker, the pen-name of a young writer from New Jersey, who started his writing journey with play-writing. He has always been fascinated with the psychology of murderers and how the media might play a role in their creation. James loves to constantly test out new styles and ideas in his writing so one day he can find something cool and unique to himself.

Brenda Brown is a writer and an illustrator-cartoonist. Her art can be found in books distributed both nationally and internationally. She has also written many books related to her graduate degree in psychology and her minor in history. Like many true crime enthusiasts, she loves exploring the minds of those who see the world as a playground for expressing the darker side of themselves—the side that people usually locked up and hid from scrutiny.

Genoveva Ortiz is a Los Angeles-based writer who began her career writing scary stories while still in college. After receiving a B.A. in English in 2018, she shifted her focus to nonfiction and the real-life horrors of crime and unsolved mysteries. Together with True Crime Seven, she is excited to further explore the world of true crime through a social justice perspective.

You can learn more about us and our writers at:

https://truecrimeseven.com/about/

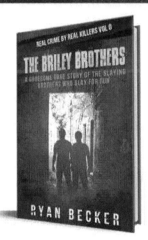

Dark Fantasies Turned Reality

Prepare yourself, we're not going to **hold back on details or cut out any of the gruesome truths...**

Made in the USA
Columbia, SC
29 February 2020